COVID: Hindsight is "2020"

How Trump *Saved* Two Million Americans from COVID-19

Jonathon Moseley, Esq.
Executive Director
of the
White House Defense Fund

Did President Trump Save Two Million Americans?

A Citizen Resource Guide to Defend Truth

Written by Jonathon A. Moseley
Executive Director, White House Defense Fund
www.WhiteHouseDefense.org

Publication Date: September 28, 2020
(updated October 7, 2020)

Cover Photo credit: Shutterstock, purchased
Cover Design, Graphics, and Creation:
Spencer Grahl Design -- Georgia

Media Inquiries: (703) 656-1230 (EST)
contact@jonmoseley.com

Bulk sales for events or projects encouraged

TABLE OF CONTENTS

TABLE OF CONTENTS iii
About the Author v
Acknowledgements vi
Request for Donations vii
Dedication viii
Foreword (Involuntary) 1
What Exactly is The Question? 2
Update: Mask-Wearing Virginia Governor Catches
    Virus Exactly One Week Before Trump.............6
Opponents Blame President for a Virus 15
Trump Acted Quickly to Fight COVID-19: *It's an
    Emergency"* 20
Life Long "Germophobe" President Warned the
    Nation Against New Virus: Updated October
    2020: 44
Democrat-Run New York City was the Inferno that
    Fueled Epidemic Nation-wide 51
When Should Trump Have Started Acting? 58
The World Health Organization Said Don't Worry
    About It 88
Trump Saved Two Million Lives 94
No, Trump Never Said The Virus Is A Hoax 102
NO, Trump Did Not Fire The Pandemic Response
    Team 111
Impeachment Managers "Have Blood On Their
    Hands"...125
Trump Gave Reassuring Hope will Taking Strong
    action..129
Consult Your Doctor for Medical Advice and
    Information 139
The Disease Is Not The Virus The Virus Is Not The
    Disease 143

National Mandate To WEar Universally-Required Masks? 154
Medical Supplies And Personal Protective Equipment: A Disaster Of Globalist Dependence On China 175
Trump's "Slow" Testing Efforts? 182
NO USA Did Not Refuse Tests From The World Health Organization 187
Covid-19 Is Mostly A Democrat Problem, Not Trump's Fault...193
China's Suppression Of Information Hindered Response 197
Conclusion 212
Bibliography / End Notes 215

ABOUT THE AUTHOR

Jonathon Moseley is Executive Director of the White House Defense Fund. He has been a Virginia business and criminal defense attorney since 1997 in private practice and as in-house counsel.

Moseley also has many years of conservative political activism. He started as co-chairman on the University of Florida campus of the 1984 Reagan-Bush campaign, appointed by Chairman Anthony Ring. He promoted anti-missile defenses and peace through strength at the Center for Peace and Freedom and High Frontier. He worked with many Republican election campaigns, including as Campaign Manager and Treasurer for Christine O'Donnell in 2008 for U.S. Senate in Delaware and Treasurer of Karen Testerman's Senate campaign.

Jon Moseley worked for Judicial Watch assisting with political transparency cases and good government litigation. As in-house counsel for a Virginia company he won new precedent for taxes. Since 2014, he worked again for Larry Klayman at Klayman's new organization Freedom Watch.

Moseley is a member of the Northern Virginia Tea Party and has published over a hundred political columns. He was a co-host with the Conservative Commandos Radio Show. He provides a weekly segment on Action Radio.

Moseley spent 5 years working at the U.S. Department of Education trying to improve our schools, including at the Center for Choice in Education ("The Lost Years"), before going to law school at George Mason University. He holds a degree in finance from the University of Florida.

Acknowledgements

This edition was published with practical help of Freedom Publishers. Thanks for practical and financial assistance, and advice and participation to: Associate Editor: Owen Jones, Executive Editor: Hanover Henry and staff. (**www.FreedomPublishers.com**)

COVID: Hindsight is "2020" is written by Jonathon A. Moseley, stimulated by our efforts at the White House Defense Fund to fight the unprecedented attacks on the institution of the Presidency, threatening to harm our country.

I thank my brother James Moseley, who paved the way by publishing his own books. He assisted me in technical steps of publishing this one. I thank my sister including for the title. I thank family and friends who nit-picked my writing over many years, making me frustrated but a much better writer.

Moseley has agreed with the U.S. Public Policy Council for the White House Defense Fund to freely distribute a shorter version "Big Lies" by mail. The author does not receive a salary from WHDF but occasional minor payments for isolated projects.

The organizations helping distribute this book do not advocate for or against candidates for local, state or federal office. But I sure do.

Request for Donations

Although the author is selling this book as a standard author as the copyright owner, the **Freedom Center Foundation** provided a grant for expenses of production, publication, and promotion such as the cover design. This was especially needed due to the incredibly short turn-around time and fast action needed since the onset of the plague of falsehoods as well as the actual viral plague. Getting this book out so fast was challenging and tough.

The Freedom Center Foundation is seeking tax-deductible donations for their work in general and on this book. Especially, they propose to pay for the printing of at least 1,000 copies of this book to be distributed to the 535 members of Congress as well as journalists, talk show hosts, etc. You may contact them at: Chairman@FreedomCenterFoundation.org

The Freedom Center Foundation is an IRS Code 501(c)(3) non-profit and tax deductible organization. Freedom Center, Post Office Box 820, Stuarts Draft, Virginia 24477-0820.

The White House Defense Fund is a project of the United States Public Policy Council, an IRS Code 501(c)(4) public policy corporation. However, donations to a 501(c)(4) public policy organization are not tax deductible.

DEDICATION

While there could be so many choices, this book is dedicated to Christine O'Donnell, former candidate for U.S. Senate from Delaware. But that is not for any of the reasons some may imagine but because her 2010 campaign exposed the same dishonest smears and attacks we are seeing today and revealed the tactics and mentality of the Republican establishment. *__We must learn this.__*

The smears today against President Donald Trump and many other leaders were road-tested against tea party leaders like Joe Miller in Alaska, Michelle Bachman, Sharon Angle, and Christine O'Donnell. The same outrageously-false smears and deceptions were practiced against many victims. The lying mainstream media, establishment, and Leftist revolutionaries were sharpening their knives.

We must recognize that the Left (of both major parties) runs the same scams again and again, just scratching out the name from last time and replacing a new name. *__Notice recurring patterns.__*

When the Left-wing establishment of both parties says exactly the same things, just changing the name they attack, can we take anything they say seriously? That is why we must never forget, never forgive, these vicious attacks on conservative leaders. The patterns teach us not to fall for scams.

It is a formula. It is a template. It's a scam.

We've seen this movie before. By the time Donald Trump challenged the powers that be, the Leftist establishment had perfected the vicious attacks and lies. It is not about the victim. It is about liars who don't care whom they injure, one after another, in their mad lust for power.

Did President Trump Save Two Million Americans?

The Republican who ran for U.S. Senate from Delaware *before* Christine lost by a 41% margin. The Republican who ran for Senate *after* Christine lost by a 37% margin. Christine lost in 2010 by a 17% margin. Delaware Republicans routinely lose statewide for other offices by about the same 17% margin year after year. (Kevin Wade did better his second time, only slightly better than Christine.) On November 1, 2008, "moderate" Republican powerhouse John McCain was on the same ballot for President on the same day that Christine was on the ballot for U.S. Senate against Joe Biden. McCain – in the national news for decades -- got roughly the same percentage of the vote that day in Delaware as Christine did. (Yes, Ann Coulter: by-gone, tired ole man Castle would have lost by 30%.)

Yet does the establishment attack the Republican who lost for U.S. Senate by a 41% margin? Or the Republican who lost by a 37% margin for U.S. Senate? Of course not. Let's pick on the one who lost in a blue State by the *smallest* margin. Because that's what liars do. They are not interested in truth.

Whom did the liars smear? You got it. The young, attractive, smart, talented woman who threatened the Left's narrative that women and young people vote Democrat. Any candidate who threatens to expose the false narratives must be destroyed. From self-achiever African-American Clarence Thomas to attractive, charismatic women like Palin, O'Donnell, and Bachman, they might persuade a new generation to leave the bankrupt Leftist con game. Those whom the Leftist establishment of both parites "must destroy" reveal whom they fear the most. ***It is never personal, any wrong done by their target. It is always a scam***.

Foreword (Involuntary)

Statement by Governor Andrew
Cuomo of New York before Campaign

> "So I will call the President. He has been helpful to New York in the past. And he has moved very quickly in the past. I am going to ask if he can make this adjustment for us because it would be truly beneficial."
>
> -- N.Y. Governor Andrew Cuomo
> Press Conference, April 6, 2020, at time 12:18, *(emphasis added)*
> CNBC, https://www.youtube.com/watch?v=K033NDQbC3A?t=575 [1]
>
> "We like to think that we can control everything. We can't. We like to think that we can fix everything. And fix all the problems for people. We can't. ... That's Mother Nature."
>
> -- *Id.* at time 19:05, onward

WHAT EXACTLY IS THE QUESTION?

This book documents the truth from hard sources:

Trump acted quickly, strongly, and effectively – when experts were telling the public there was nothing to worry about.

It is sadly predictable that those who criticize Trump today for allegedly acting too slowly, criticized him then for acting too quickly.

So what is our debate question? "Resolved that … xyz…" What is being disputed?

To examine if a president acted quickly and strongly enough, we have to ask:

- when was the starting point, when a President should have started acting?
- and then what exactly _did_ this President _actually_ do and when?

The smears and attacks against us, the voters, who dared to elect the wrong President, are all based on foggy, vague, confusing claims lacking in specifics. If we shine a light on the details, a different story emerges. The lies are exposed.

So, when – exactly -- should President Trump or any other President have recognized that minor action needed to be taken? Or when should much more serious, major action have been started?

At different stages in the unfolding events, when should a pandemic have been treated as a public health emergency, a threatening pandemic, a crisis?

These are different stages, at different points in time. On what dates did the spreading COVID-19 [2] disease reach each different level of severity in the threat? At which date did COVID-19 require a different level of response? You can't talk about just one date, as rumors swirled within Wuhan and Hubei Province, denied and suppressed by China's government, then finally the truth started to leak out, and the virus was only in Hubei Province, and then infected people started to flee to Italy, Iran, etc.

And then on the other side of the analysis: When did this President start to act? What did Trump do and how quickly? Those who want to accuse Trump of killing people because of a disease offer inaccurate starting points at which a prudent President should have started to act and when this President actually did act.

You have to watch the facts to notice the lies. The critics of the president seeking to pervert the facts and history hide behind vague, ambiguous statements as usual.

Critics imply that Trump was warned in November or December (not true) or in January (only at the end of January, not at the beginning).

Then they argue that Trump did nothing until … well, not clear… late. When? We guess March.

That's not true either.

It was not until Kamala Harris' debate with Mike Pence that she gave away the game. **January 28, 2020**. [3] That was the date Harris identified as when Trump should have realized that COVID-19 on the other side of the planet was airborne and presented a danger. Harris made the mistake of being specific when the anti-Trump position depends upon a cloud of fog and lies.

But Donald Trump started shutting down travel from China on **January 17, 2020**. Trump created an intergovernmental task force on January 27, 2020. Trump declared a national public health emergency on January 31, 2020 and shut down travel from China. So by Harris' own standard, Trump succeeded and acted properly.

The hard facts in this book will prove that Harris is wrong. As late as February 29, 2020, public health experts were pronouncing publicly that there was little risk to America from COVID-19.

As late as **March 2, 2020**, through **March 5, 2020**, New York City's Health Commissioner (a highly-trained physician) assured New Yorkers that there was little risk of COVID-19 to New Yorkers because the virus SARS-CoV-2 cannot be spread by casual contact. The doctor said that, not me. NYC's Health Commissioner was advising the nation's #1 hotspot that causal contact cannot spread the virus. She was wrong. But that was as late as March 5, 2020.

The expert opinions were a swirl of chaos and conflicting opinions until March 11, 202, when even the World Health Organization finally admitted COVID-19 is a pandemic (previously a matter of health "concern").

Some of the following chapters present a timeline of some highlights of what the Trump Administration did to respond to the natural disaster of a disease known as COVID-19. Some details of New York have been moved out into a chapter.

The next chapter (after the update) is in order of earliest of the highlights to the latest in time, to show how the Trump Administration acted early and strongly. (Surely there are behind the scenes inside government there were surely earlier actions taken but these are the conspicuous publicly-known actions.)

The second chapter after that (after the germophobe president) one is in reverse order, from the latest in time to the earliest to show that as late as March 5, 2020, there was significant uncertainty how serious or not the COVID-19 outbreak in China might be.

Experts in the U.S. public health community and international organizations, including Dr. Anthony Fauci, kept telling the American people again and again that ***the risk to the American people is low***, in various ways, in various times. Again and again.

At worst, experts expressed uncertainty about whether there was any danger to the American people from the virus spreading in China, **up through the transitional time period of February 25, 2020, through March 11, 2020**.

It was not until February 25, 2020, that the expert opinion *began* to turn – still with mixed messages until March 11, 2020.

These were *not* Trump's positions. Those were the declarations of national and international non-partisan, public health professionals.

The experts. The science.

The tide of opinion was turning from February 25 to March 11, like the harbor tide changing direction, still mixed and churning.

But there was no uniform consensus clearly seeing a real problem until March 11, 2020

Update: Mask-Wearing Virginia Governor Catches Virus Exactly One Week Before Trump

Update: Very early on October 2, 2020, President Trump announced by tweet that he and the First Lady Melania Trump had tested infected for COVID-19.

The political world and the news media immediately began to blame Trump for not having taken the virus seriously. He brought this on himself, the Left crowed.

Oh, and we hope he dies. Facebook said that they will remove posts wishing for anyone to die or celebrating Trump's infection. But they don't.

Now, President Trump and his medical staff report that he is feeling fine and his brief experiences with some symptoms are now gone.

Donald and Melania Trump have access to the best medical care including the most cutting-edge medicines and treatments.   He has tolerated hydroxychloroquine well in the past without side effects for the recommended two week course. If it becomes necessary, Trump will be given hydroxychloroquine or other medications.

None of these are available without a doctor's prescription.   Doctors make these decisions. Treating COVID-19 is not a "do it yourself" project. The President's doctors will decide.

The probability is almost 100% that Trump will recover. There is always the risk of a sudden and catastrophic cytokine storm damaging the lining of the lungs. But – although tragic – that is unlikely.

Although COVID-19 is not influenza, it is informative to make some comparisons.   Like someone recovering from the flu, we expect Trump to be in high spirits most of the day, but he probably will drag for a few weeks, like any person at the tail end of the flu. No, COVID-19 is not the flu. But the similarity does give us insights what to expect.

A number of people could have been infected with SARS-CoV-2 at the announcement event of Trump's nomination of Judge Amy Coney Barrett to the Supreme Court. Maybe. Could be. Is that what passes for news? Rank speculation?

But we have also learned that *before* the September 26 event Barrett announcement, the White House Chief of Security, Mr. Crede Bailey, came down with a severe case of COVID-19. [4] So the virus must have been in the White House long before the Barrett event. Bailey was both running security for the White House grounds but highly contagious with a severe case.

But here is the scam: There is always a scam with the Left, the news media, and the D.C. Swamp:

Trump does not wear a mask when speaking from a podium. They say Trump is against masks.

On October 6, 2020, when Trump walked up onto the Truman Balcony with its magnificent visuals at the White House, he took off his mask in celebration of being home from Walter Reed hospital. [5] He was following the science. You don't need a mask when standing alone on a balcony far from anyone else, outdoors.

As the Associated Press admitted on September 17, 2020, while otherwise smearing the President: [6]

> The CDC recommended in April that people wear cloth face coverings in public when it's difficult to be socially distant.

Got that? The CDC recommended face masks *"when it's difficult to be socially distant."*

Now contrast Trump with Virginia's Democrat Governor Ralph Northam. This is an important way to help busy people quickly and vividly "get it."

September 25, 2020 – Virginia's obsessively mask-wearing Northam and his wife Pamela test infected for the SARS-CoV-2 virus.

In an exact parallel to the President and First Lady, Virginia's Governor and First Lady had the exact same diagnosis *only about one week earlier:* [7]

> "Northam, 61, a former Army doctor and pediatrician, has required Virginians to wear masks inside public spaces during the pandemic. He also has urged frequent hand-washing and social distancing."

> "As I have been reminding Virginians throughout this crisis, #COVID19 is very real and very contagious," he tweeted Friday. "We are grateful for your thoughts and support, but the best thing you can do for us — and most importantly, for your fellow Virginians — is to take this virus seriously."

This author is a Virginia attorney. In Virginia, no one can enter any store or office or government building without wearing a face mask. Yet Virginia's "Governor Mask" caught the SARS-CoV-2 virus one week before President Trump did.

Then, October 2, 2020 – *One week later*: President Donald Trump, falsely smeared as opposed to masks, and his wife Melania test infected for the SARS-CoV-2 virus. [8]

> President Trump revealed early Friday morning that he and the first lady, Melania Trump, had tested positive for the coronavirus, throwing the nation's leadership into uncertainty and escalating the crisis posed by a pandemic that has already killed more than 207,000 Americans and devastated the economy.

The Washington Post defended Virginia's Democrat Governor, after Northam became infected with the SARS-CoV-2 virus.

> Northam has tried to chart a nuanced path through the pandemic, imposing strict restrictions early on to try to contain the virus while easing up in some areas ahead of neighboring Maryland and D.C.

Nuanced? Well, Virginia was not among the first states to be completely shut down, but the restrictions then became very severe. And when Virginia went into partial re-opening, Northam ordered the transition by *expanding* – not relaxing – the requirement to wear masks.

Yet Virginia's Governor still caught COVID-19, despite meticulous and obsessive mask-wearing. Did a lack of wearing masks cause President Trump to catch COVID-19? No. Northam caught it while wearing masks all the time (after getting caught and criticized in May for going to beach once maskless).

When Joe Biden gave a press conference in a Delaware corn field, more than 100 feet away from anyone else, Biden did not wear a mask. [9] That is the expert guidance: Wear a mask only if you cannot keep a safe distance. Or if you really feel like it, sure, go ahead. Do more, if you want.

I am watching the Today show, the morning "news" show on NBC. Four performers, called "journalists," are sitting on stools *without masks on.* Their stools are about 10 feet away from each other in the studio. But none of them are wearing COVID-19 masks. None of them. October, 2020.

That is the correct "science."

Turn on TV news. See the anchor? Behind the camera you are watching through stands a cameraman. Out of your view, there are probably three cameras for the control booth to cut to. That's three cameramen. There is a studio floor director in the studio with the "journalist." Someone is manning the intense lighting. There are staff workers ushering guests. But the journalists are not wearing masks on set, on camera. They are at least 6 to 10 feet away from anyone else in the studio. That's the science. That's what Trump is doing.

But Trump is against masks, they falsely accuse, because Trump follows the same guidance they do.

The initial guidance was don't wear masks at all. All the public health experts insisted that masks don't work – the experts' words, not mine. Note how the dishonest Associated Press tried mightily to smear Trump in the September 17 piece:

> In June, as he prepared to hold his first indoor political rally of the COVID era, Trump complained to The Wall Street Journal that people can't help

> but fidget with the coverings, similar to assertions he made on national television this week.

> "They put their finger on the mask, and they take them off, and then they start touching their eyes and touching their nose and their mouth," Trump said in his Journal interview. "And then they don't know how they caught it?"

No, that was not Trump's crazy ideas. Trump was repeating exactly what Dr. Fauci and all of the public health experts were saying before April. This is why the Surgeon General told us *not* to buy or wear masks as late as February 29, 2020.

Infectious disease expert Dr. Anthony Fauci told 60 Minutes on March 8, 2020: [10]

> "Right now people should not be wearing... there is no reason to be walking around with a mask. When you are in the middle of an outbreak wearing a mask might make people feel a little bit better and it might even block a droplet. But it is not providing the perfect protection that people think it is. And often there are unintended consequences. People keep fiddling with the mask, and they keep touching their face."

What the Associated Press quotes Trump as saying – portraying it as something crazy – is almost word for word what St. Fauci told 60

Did President Trump Save Two Million Americans?

Minutes in early March. And many other public health officials were saying the same thing:

U.S. Surgeon General
@Surgeon_General

Seriously people- STOP BUYING MASKS!

They are NOT effective in preventing general public from catching #Coronavirus, but if healthcare providers can't get them to care for sick patients, it puts them and our communities at risk!
bit.ly/37Ay6Cm

7:08 AM · Feb 29, 2020 · Twitter for iPhone

62K Retweets and comments   **77.7K** Likes

The same AP story further lies about Trump, arguing that:

> WASHINGTON (AP) — White House officials insist that President Donald Trump strongly supports face masks to prevent the spread of coronavirus and always has. But the president's own words and actions tell a very different — and sometimes puzzling — story.

The AP went on to lie some more, by quoting some dishonest experts:

> Dr. Tom Inglesby, director of the Center for Health Security at the Johns Hopkins Bloomberg School of Public Health, said he's "bewildered" by Trump's ambiguity about masks. He said widespread use would also help

restore economic vitality faster, a prime Trump goal.

"I don't think that there's any controversy about masks anywhere in the world," Inglesby said. "Why we continue to have this debate about it is a mystery."

Maybe because Dr. Fauci and the Surgeon General told us all *not* to wear masks? How is that Trump's fault? Trump is to blame because the experts can't agree with each other or even agree with themselves from one day to the next?

And there is no ambiguity. Just because there is more than one step in the logic should not leave an expert "bewildered." Let's be honest: Do we really think that Dr. Tom Inglesby, director of the Center for Health Security at the Johns Hopkins Bloomberg School of Public Health is completely unaware that the CDC advised wearing a mask only when social distancing is not possible or practical?

When Trump is speaking from a podium with adequate distance from everyone else, Trump does the correct thing according to the experts:

Trump does not wear a mask if he can engage in anti-social distancing. That's the correct science.

But it's our fault that we are left scratching our heads. We don't follow the "science" through dizzying paths of flips and flops. Have you heard these public health "experts" apologize for giving us the wrong guidance up through April?

So then the guidance changed to *either* stay at an anti-social distance *or* wear a mask – not both. Trump is doing it correctly. Trump is not wearing a mask from the podium. Trump repeatedly says he has a mask in his pocket at all times in case he gets into a situation where anti-social distancing is not possible.

Furthermore, the science has always been that you should wear a mask when around the general public. The CDC guidance acknowledges that when you are in your own house among your own family, the mask is pointless and useless. The mask is not going to make any difference with the people you live with in the same house.

Furthermore, the blue rectangle masks are disposable. Periodically *__YOU MUST THROW THEM AWAY__* and *__PUT ON A NEW MASK.__* Doctors and nurses do not wear the same mask for weeks. These become itchy, because the inside is frayed and worn. *Throw it away and get a new one!*

For more permanent N95 masks or cloth masks, wash them frequently with thorough sterilization.

OPPONENTS BLAME
PRESIDENT FOR A VIRUS

Sorry, but we are talking about a disease here. The coronavirus SARS-CoV-2 is essentially a natural disaster, like a hurricane, a tornado, a flood, or a forest fire.

As Governor Andrew Cuomo admitted on April 6, before the virus became totally politicized:

> **"We like to think that we can control everything. We can't. We like to think that we can fix everything. And fix all the problems for people. We can't. ... That's Mother Nature."**

-- N.Y. Governor Andrew Cuomo, Press Conference, April 6, 2020, t time 19:05, onward [11]

Yet, the Boston Globe claims [12] that President Donald Trump has "blood on his hands" because a virus spread out of China. The global coronavirus pandemic is a world-changing event. The crisis is also a major turning point in our nation's political life and the future of our country.

What will you need to know and how will you need to fight, if you care about the direction our country will take and you care about truth and facts?

On September 17, 2020 in a CNN town hall, Joe Biden stated: [13]

> "If the president had done his job, had done his job from the beginning, all the people would still be alive. All the

people. I'm not making this up. Just look at the data."

"60% of Democratic voters now blame Trump not China for coronavirus crisis: Poll," explained *The Washington Times* headline on April 20, 2020.[14] And:

> "The coronavirus pandemic has sparked a partisan blame game. Most Democratic voters — 60% — now blame President Trump rather than China, for the health emergency now underway nationwide, according to a Rasmussen Reports survey [15] released Monday. Among all voters, 42% also pointed the finger at the president."

> "[M]ost say their governor is doing a better job than President Trump in handling the coronavirus outbreak," according to The Hill [16] and a Harvard university public opinion poll of 22,000 voters. "But on a state-by-state basis, respondents said they approve of the job their governors are doing to respond to the outbreak more than they approve of the job Trump is doing in every state and the District of Columbia."

Nancy Pelosi calls the coronavirus SARS-CoV-2 the "Trump virus." [17] Partisan propagandists claim that President Donald Trump did not act promptly to respond to the disease. Had Trump acted sooner, people would not have died. This was a major theme of the Democrat National Convention and is becoming the main issue in the presidential election.

The D.C. Swamp is cynically exploiting this human tragedy. Rep. Adam Schiff (D-CA) and others are setting up a commission[18] "like 9/11" to investigate President Donald Trump's handling of the COVID-19 coronavirus. "House Speaker Nancy Pelosi said on CNN's "State of the Union"[19] that Congress would review the Trump administration's handling of the pandemic .... What did he know and when did he know it? That's for an after-action review. But as the President fiddles, people are dying," Pelosi said.[20]

As the Associated Press reported,[21] "The chairman of the House Homeland Security Committee, Rep. Bennie Thompson, D-Miss., and the chairman of the House Intelligence Committee, Rep. Adam Schiff, D-Calif., are working on separate bills establishing a commission." They only care about squeezing political advantage [22] out of every tragedy.

Left-wing activists on social media are essentially accusing Trump of murder. Their logic goes like this: A disease killed people. Trump is President. Therefore Trump killed 214,081 people.

A group of bitter, establishment Republicans in Name Only (RINOs) – whom the voters rejected in favor of an outsider agent of change – have started an organization called The Lincoln Project.

They are running internet ads and a website claiming that *(I will not give a link to help them)* –

> Because Donald Trump chose to lie to us instead of protecting us, we have lost over 200,000 friends, neighbors, community members, and loved ones.

We have lost precious time and memories we will never get back.

They are attacking Trump with such "dignified" smears, not divisive at all, claiming:

DONALD TRUMP IS KILLING US

In times of crisis, we rely on our leaders to protect and defend us. Instead, Donald Trump has chosen to lie to us and kill us.

These are the "dignified" establishment insiders. Not divisive at all, right? This is the ugly, dishonest, nasty Republican establishment that the American people have suffered since 1964. Their horrible attacks on Trump – including attacking him for not being dignified – are nothing new. Just ask Christine O'Donnell or Sarah Palin.

Apparently these RINOs think that Abraham Lincoln wasn't controversial, even with the vicious attacks on Lincoln during his first and second election campaign. These RINOs are campaigning for the party of slavery and the party whose follower assassinated Lincoln.

Hillary Clinton in her speech at the Democrat National Convention blamed COVID-19 deaths on Trump. Heck, everyone at the Convention spent much of their time trying to argue (with fuzzy words) that because people died, therefore Donald Trump killed them.

Regardless of whether one approves or disapproves of Donald Trump individually or as President of the United States, cynical opportunists are deviously deceiving the public, rewriting history, and distorting reality.

On the important public policy issue facing our nation and our world of the Coronavirus pandemic, reality is being ripped apart by dishonest politicians who want to offer an alternate reality. Not only does this distort decision-making today but it will set up a false narrative for decades into the future.

They can't be serious, can they? Can a president – any president – control a disease? I know of only one person in human history who could command disease to vanish (although He told His followers to likewise heal in His name).

And the establishment when He walked the Earth crucified Jesus out of jealousy for how the average people, the Forgotten Man, loved and responded to Jesus rather than to them.

In the United States, we elect a President, not a God, every four years. Only a Leftist, because Leftists worship government, would confuse an elected official with God.

Yet critics of this President – really any Republican President – are trying to blame a secular governmental official, the chief administrator and manager of the Executive Branch of our government, for a disease that was spawned in China.

TRUMP ACTED QUICKLY TO FIGHT COVID-19: *"IT'S AN EMERGENCY"*

Attacks on the President falsely claim that he started to act in March after he was warned in November or December. These key dates are just false. Critics deceptively confuse the President's attempts to calm and reassure the public with not taking action. One can speak softly and work fast.

Everyone faced with this fake controversy must ask the following question: If Trump had done more, **what**? *What could a president have done that Trump did not already do*?

We have critics like Joe Biden who propose what they would do to fight COVID-19.

But, curiously, their plans are what Donald Trump already did. So... sorry, too late.

So what could any president do that President Donald Trump did not already do, early, and strongly? [23]

Bottom line "take away" – What part of *EMERGENCY* do people fail to understand?

On **January 31, 2020**, President Trump declared a *PUBLIC HEALTH EMERGENCY*, through the Secretary of Health and Human Services Alex Azar.

If the American people would not understand the declaration of an *EMERGENCY* on January 31, 2020, what else was supposed to tip them off that COVID-19 was a serious threat?

On **January 31, 2020**, [24] Trump ordered and announced a declaration of a public health emergency [25] for the entire United States, [26] through the U.S. Department of Health and Secretary Alex M. Azar. [27]

"We are committed to

protecting the health and safety of all Americans, and this public health emergency declaration is the latest in the series of steps the Trump Administration has taken to protect our country," Secretary Azar said. [28]

The emergency declaration [29] gave authority to assign government and public health personnel anywhere in the country to respond to the threat. Trump activated the complete public health and health care powers and systems of the U.S. Government.[30] While Trump did not declare a more-typical natural disaster emergency until **March 31, 2020**, [31] the public health emergency was what was needed in January. That is what was actually relevant to the problem.

As chronicled in The Federalist, [32] "On **January 17**, the CDC and the Department of Homeland Security (DHS) announced that American citizens returning from travel-restricted countries were being rerouted [diverted] to specific airports, where they would be screened and isolated."

On **January 20, 2020**, Dr. Anthony Fauci announced [33] that the National Institutes of Health was already working on the development of a vaccine for the coronavirus.

In **January**, Trump assembled a $105 million special task force to guide the anti-virus crusade.

In **February**, the Administration signed up a company to work on a vaccine.

On **January 21, 2020**, Trump activated the CDC's Emergency Operations Center to better provide ongoing support to the COVID-19 response. [34]

On **January 23, 2020**, Trump continued to phase in further restrictions to implement a growing shut down of travel from China. [35]

On **January 27, 2020**, Trump established a national task force to coordinate efforts to fight the virus, which was announced on January 29. [36]

As early as **January 27, 2020**, the Trump Administration was aggressively responding to the coronavirus spreading from Wuhan, China, and Hubei Province, more than a month before the first COVID-19 death of anyone actually infected within the United States (as opposed to getting infected overseas and then returning home already sick) and more than two weeks before Europe counted its first death of anyone who became infected anywhere within the European continent. However, there were only 110 people being tracked as potentially having COVID-19 as of January 27, 2020. [37]

> More than 100 people in 26 states are being monitored for the new coronavirus that has killed 81 people in China, a U.S. health official said Monday.
>
> The news comes as the CDC on Monday raised its travel alert level for China to level 3, meaning Americans should avoid nonessential travel to the entire nation.
>
> Nancy Messonnier, director of the National Center for Immunization and Respiratory Diseases, said 110 people are "under investigation" for the virus but added that human-to-human `

transmission of the virus has not been documented in the U.S.

"This is a rapidly changing situation, both here and abroad," Messonnier said. "However, the immediate risk to the general U.S. public is low at this time."

Still, she said a program for screening travelers entering the U.S. from Wuhan could be expanded in the coming days to include other parts of China. President Donald Trump tweeted Monday that U.S. officials are in "very close communication" with China and offered aid to President Xi Jinping as his nation grapples with the coronavirus.

* * *

China's confirmed cases have ballooned to more than 2,800 since the coronavirus was discovered last month. The epicenter of the outbreak is Wuhan, a city of 11 million people, but more than 40 cases have been confirmed in a dozen other countries, including five in the U.S.

"All US cases traveled from Wuhan," the Centers for Disease Control and Prevention said in a statement. "More cases may be identified. However, risk to US general public is still considered low."

In the U.S., two cases have been confirmed in California, one in Arizona, one in Illinois and one in Washington State. Dozens of cities and states continue to screen patients whose symptoms are consistent with the virus.

Drug companies are racing the clock to develop a vaccine.

On **January 27, 2020**, President Trump clearly raised a warning about the COVID-19 coronavirus to the American people, public officials, and his more than 80 million Twitter followers including journalists and public health officials and the medical community around the world.

Donald J. Trump @realDonaldTrump

We are in very close communication with China concerning the virus. Very few cases reported in USA, but strongly on watch. We have offered China and President Xi any help that is necessary. Our experts are extraordinary!

9:56 AM · Jan 27, 2020 · Twitter for iPhone

21.4K Retweets   1.5K Quote Tweets   115.6K Likes

Tweet

By **January 31, 2020**, the Centers for Disease Control and Prevention were already working with state health departments on disease surveillance, contact tracing, and providing interim guidance for clinicians on identifying and treating coronavirus infections. Yes, critics, contact tracing was started.

On the same day, **January 31, 2020**, Trump ordered restrictions on travel from China[38] including [39] that "foreign nationals who recently visited China won't be allowed to enter the U.S., and American citizens returning from mainland China will be subject to 14-day quarantines." Trump's travel restrictions ordered that people recently in infected areas may not enter, other than U.S. citizens returning home.[40] The 195 citizens [41] returning from Wuhan, China were ordered into quarantine upon returning to the U.S.A. [42]

On **February 4, 2020**, Trump ordered the Food and Drug Administration [43] to streamline and accelerate coronavirus diagnostic testing procedures, including dismantling outdated procedures and regulations he discovered were hindering the effort.

As noted below, in his state of the union address on **February 4, 2020**, President Trump promised to take strong, effective action against the coronavirus on February 4, 2020. [44] Trump explained that: "My administration will take all necessary steps to safeguard our citizens from this threat."

As early as on **February 5, 2020**, the FDA rushed emergency approval of a coronavirus diagnostic test. [45]

> The Food and Drug Administration issued an expedited approval of a test for the new coronavirus, signing off on its use by state health labs. That should speed up efforts in the US to detect cases of the virus, which has sickened nearly 25,000 people around

the world. Until now, all samples from suspected cases in the US had to be sent to the Centers for Disease Control and Prevention for testing.

The FDA sidestepped the usual regulatory channels and signed off on the test under an Emergency Use Authorization, which allows the use of medical products in life-threatening situations when no approved alternatives are available. The agency previously issued emergency authorizations for tests for MERS, Ebola, and Zika.

So far, 260 people have been under investigation for the coronavirus in the United States. Only 11 have been confirmed positive, and 167 have tested negative. The remaining 82 cases are still pending. The test only takes between four and six hours to run, but it can take significantly more time for state health departments to ship samples to the CDC central lab in Atlanta, Georgia. Now, state labs will be able to run the tests themselves, speeding up the process.

* * *

"To start, around 200 test kits will be sent to qualified domestic and international labs, and each kit can run around 700 to 800 coronavirus tests."

For quarantine, already well before **February 11, 2020**, more than 200 U.S. citizen evacuees from China were living under federal quarantine at the Marine Corps Air Station Miramar in San Diego. [46]

On **February 24, 2020**, before the first death of anyone in the United States who became infected domestically, instead of being infected overseas and returning home, the Trump administration sent a letter to Congress, requesting a funding commitment of at least $2.5 billion to help combat the spread of the novel coronavirus, including to replenish funds and stockpiles used for EBOLA. [47]

> Office of Management and Budget spokesperson Rachel Semmel said in a statement to Axios that the Trump administration was transmitting to Congress a $2.5 billion supplemental funding plan 'to accelerate vaccine development, support preparedness and response activities and to procure much-needed equipment and supplies'
>
> We are also freeing up existing resources and allowing for greater flexibilities for response activities," Semmel said.
>
> The HHS said in a statement it intended to provide resources to continue the department's "robust and multi-layered public health preparedness and response efforts — including public health surveillance, epidemiology, laboratory testing, support for state and local

governments and other key partners, advanced research and development of new vaccines, therapeutics and diagnostics, advanced manufacturing enhancements, and support for the Strategic National Stockpile.

The funding would cover more than $1 billion for vaccines, therapeutics, vaccine development and stockpiling of personal protective equipment, such as masks. *Id.*

On **February 24, 2020**, the corresponding letter [48] sent to Task Force leader Mike Pence and to Congressional leadership also explained the progress being made by the Trump Administration:

The Government has taken unprecedented steps to minimize the risk of travelers spreading COVID-19 to the United States. The President suspended entry into the United States of certain foreign nationals who have recently traveled to China and who pose a risk of transmitting the virus and directed inbound flights from China to 11 airports where enhanced screening now takes place.

The Government has conducted numerous charter flights to evacuate American citizens from Wuhan, in the Hubei Province, China and the cruise ship *Diamond Princess* back to the United States. All passengers were screened for symptoms before the flights, and medical professionals

continue to monitor the health of all
returning passengers.

* * *

***However, much is still unknown
about this virus and the disease it
causes.***

(Emphasis added).

On **February 27, 2020**, Director of the CDC
Robert R. Redfield, M.D. testified before a U.S.
House of Representatives Foreign Affairs
subcommittee: [49]

> As of February 20, 2020, CDC has
> deployed over 800 staff to work full
> time on the COVID-19 response,
> including those working on the
> response from CDC headquarters,
> overseas offices, and field
> deployments. This includes CDC staff
> supporting China through the CDC
> country office in Beijing, China; ….
> Beyond China, CDC is assisting
> ministries of health in countries in
> every region of the globe with their
> most urgent and immediate needs to
> prevent, detect, and respond to the
> COVID-19 outbreak. CDC's most
> expert and practiced infectious disease
> and public health experts are dedicated
> to this response 24/7 to protect the
> American people. * * * The Agency is
> using its existing epidemiologic,
> laboratory, and clinical expertise to

gain a more comprehensive understanding of COVID-19."

On **February 27, 2020**, the CDC Director also explained how CDC was taking action on the supply of masks, gowns, etc. despite reliance on China. [50]

> "... understanding the current constraints of the global supply of personal protective equipment (PPE), CDC is working with industry and the U.S. health system to comprehend possible effects on facilities' abilities to procure the needed levels of PPE, and to provide strategies to optimize the supply of PPE."

On **February 29, 2020**, Trump halted travel with Iran,[51] which was experiencing a dangerous outbreak, and increased restrictions from Italy.

On **March 12, 2020**, President Trump imposed travel restrictions on Europe [52] and elsewhere.

On **March 13, 2020**, Trump declared a National Emergency,[53] which released billions of dollars and authority under the Federal Emergency Management Agency.[54] This is different from the National Health Emergency declared January 31, 2020. This was more like a typical national disaster and released resources usually associated with national disasters like hurricanes, tornados, forest fires, earthquakes, and the like. It was the January 31, 2020, National Health Emergency declaration that was more applicable.

In fact, in a press conference on **March 12, 2020**, Dr. Anthony Fauci insisted that Trump's travel ban from China "absolutely made a difference" in protecting the United States from the disease.[55] Dr. Fauci not only confirms Trump's swift and effective action to shut down travel by anyone who had been in China recently (regardless of their immediate, last travel departure point) was the right move and worked but confirms that Trump's actions saved thousands or hundreds of thousands of lives.

On **March 13, 2020**, the Trump Administration took action to implement 1,135 regulatory waivers for state and local governments: [56]

> "Following President Trump's leadership during this health emergency, CMS is taking immediate steps to give our nation's providers, healthcare facilities, and states maximum flexibility,"

said CMS Administrator Seema Verma. "The nationwide waivers we are activating today will be a godsend for those on the frontlines of the fight against this new virus."

On **March 16, 2020**, Trump issued national guidelines [57] titled "30 Days to Slow the Spread"[58] – announcing "this is a very bad one"[59] -- which ordered nation-wide voluntary isolation at home for any one feeling sick, with children feeling sick, or living with anyone who tested positive for COVID-19, an older person, or anyone with a serious underlying health condition.

Trump issued guidelines prohibiting gatherings larger than ten people and closing restaurants, bars, and food courts in favor of drive-through, pick-up, and delivery restaurant options. The guidelines ordered avoidance of discretionary travel, shopping trips, and social visits. Visits to nursing homes, retirement, or long-term care facilities were banned except for critical assistance. And guidance for good hygiene was re-emphasized.

With these and hundreds of other actions within the details of the government, President Donald Trump acted swiftly and powerfully. But that can only be compared and understood contrasted against what was actually happening on the ground.

On **March 16, 2020**, Governor Phil Murphy [60]

> ... is essentially shutting down the state of New Jersey as the number of coronavirus cases jumped to 178 in the Garden State. All of New Jersey's public and private schools, along with colleges and universities, will close indefinitely starting Wednesday, while bars, restaurants and casinos will shutter at 8 p.m. on Monday.

As the Associated Press reported on **March 17, 2020**:

> "In a massive federal effort Tuesday, President Donald Trump asked Congress to speed emergency checks to Americans, enlisted the military for MASH-like hospitals and implored ordinary people — particularly socially active millennials — to do their part by staying home to stop the spread of the coronavirus."

> "His proposed economic package alone could approach $1 trillion, a

rescue initiative not seen since the Great Recession. Trump wants checks sent to the public within two weeks and is urging Congress to pass the eye-popping stimulus package in a matter of days." [61]

On **March 18, 2020**, Governor Andrew Cuomo described New York's partnership with President Trump and the federal government in meeting the challenge of the COVID-19 outbreak raging in New York City and New York State: [62]

> The Federal government can be extremely helpful here and we need the federal government's help.
>
> I had a conversation with the President yesterday. Uh. It was an open and honest conversation. We've always had very good dialogue. Even when we don't agree, we've always had a very good dialogue. But the President and I agreed yesterday, look, we're fighting the same war. And this is a war. And we're in the same trench. And I have your back, you have my back. We are going to do everything we can for the people of the State of New York. And the President agreed to that. And I agreed to that. And his actions demonstrate that he is doing that.
>
> I've had a number of conversations with White House staff who are working on this. I had a conversation

with the Secretary of the Army.
President sent the Army Corps of
Engineers here this afternoon. I will be
meeting with them this afternoon. I
spoke to the President this morning
about specific actions that the
President is going to take. I can tell
you who is fully engaged on trying to
help New York. He is being very
creative and very energetic. I thank
him for his partnership.

On **March 18, 2020**, Trump ordered the U.S.
Navy's two hospital ships – each with 1,000
hospital beds and a crew of 1,200 each – the *USNS
Mercy* and *USNS Comfort* to New York City harbor
and to a location off California to be chosen by that
State. [63] Like the building of a field hospital in New
York City, the hospital ships were intended to take
the pressure off of hospitals for other patients so
that the more permanent and sophisticated fully
equipped hospitals in New York City and California
can focus their expertise on COVID-19 patients.
One goal was to separate non-COVID-19 patients
onto the hospital ships to avoid them being infected
in a hospital also caring for coronavirus victims.

Defense officials noted that the
hospital ships aren't conducive to
containing infectious disease
outbreaks but can be used to treat non-
coronavirus patients while existing
medical facilities focus on disease
treatment.

"Our capabilities are focused on trauma ... they don't have necessarily the segregated spaces that you need to deal with infectious diseases," Esper said Tuesday, adding that deploying the hospital ships could "take the pressure off of civilian hospitals when it comes to trauma cases to open up civilian hospital rooms for infectious diseases."

As it turns out, New York City made almost no use of the hospital ship or the Javits center field hospital. New York State's Governor Andrew Cuomo instead ordered active COVID-19 patients into nursing homes, dramatically spreading and worsening the contagious outbreak. [64]

On **March 18, 2020**, the United States and Canada agreed to close their 5,500-mile border to nonessential traffic Wednesday, a drastic measure that officials hope will help stanch the spread of the novel coronavirus in both countries. [65]

President Trump and Canadian Prime Minister Justin Trudeau decided to close the border Wednesday morning, Trudeau said at a news conference. People will no longer be able to traverse between the two countries for recreation and tourism, Trudeau said. It was not clear when the border would reopen.

"In both our countries we're encouraging people to stay home," Trudeau said. "We're telling citizens not to visit their neighbors unless they absolutely have to. Well, this collaborative and reciprocal measure is an extension of that prudent approach."

And:

"Our governments recognize that it is critical that we preserve supply chains between both countries," Trudeau said, to "ensure food, fuel and lifesaving medicines" are able to move between the United States and Canada.

Also on **March 18, 2020**, Trump issued yet another "Executive Order on Prioritizing and Allocating Health and Medical Resources to Respond to the Spread of COVID-19." [66]

Around **March 23, 2020**, Dr. Anthony Fauci explained on Fox News [67] that the White House Coronavirus Task Force is working around the clock to fight the coronavirus outbreak. Fauci said Trump has never challenged him on the science of the coronavirus.

MARK LEVIN: Welcome back. Dr. Fauci, let me ask you a question. You've been doing this a long time. Have you ever seen this big of a coordinated response by an administration to such a threat? A health threat?

DR. ANTHONY FAUCI: Well, we've never had a threat like this, and the coordinated response has been, there are a number of adjectives to describe it. Impressive, I think is one of them.

I mean, we're talking about all-hands on-deck is that I, as one of many people on a team, I'm not the only person, since the beginning that we even recognized what this was. I have been devoting almost full time on this -- almost full time.

I'm down at the White House virtually every day with the Taskforce. I'm connected by phone throughout the day and into the night and when I say night, I'm talking twelve, one, two in the morning. I'm not the only one. There's a whole group of us that are doing that. It's every single day.

So I can't imagine that that under any circumstances that anybody could be doing more. I mean, obviously, we're fighting a formidable enemy -- this virus. This virus is a serious issue here.

Take a look at what it's done to China, to Europe, to South Korea. It is serious and our response is aimed, and I know you've heard that many, many times, and this is true. I mean, I deal with viruses my entire career.

When you have an outbreak virus, if you leave it to its own devices, it will peak up and then come back down. What we learned from China, that letting it peak up is really bad, because it can do some serious damage. So we are focused now, like a laser on doing whatever we can, and there are two or three things that deserve to be mentioned -- to make this peak actually be a mound, which means you're going to have suffering, you're going to have illness, you're going to have death. But it's not going to be the maximum that the virus can do.

A couple of ways to do that. The first was, as we say, all the time, the very timely decision on the part of the President to shut off travel from China, because we saw that there was this possibility of people coming in and seeding in the country. We did it early.

And as it turned out, there were relatively few cases in the big picture of things that came in from China. Unfortunately, for our colleagues, and many of whom are my friends and people I've trained actually in Medicine, in European countries, they didn't do that. And they got hit really hard and are being hit really hard. The first thing.

Second thing, when the infection burden shifted from China to Europe, we did the same thing with Europe. We shut off travel from Europe, which again was another safeguard to prevent influx from without in.

The other way you do it is by containment and mitigation. And now everybody knows what the word mitigation means because it's the things that we're doing. No crowds, work from home. Don't go to places that you can be susceptible. Ten people in a room, not 50 and a hundred people. Stay away from theatres.

Take the elderly people who are susceptible and have them do self-isolation. Stay out of bars, stay out of restaurants.

If you're in an area where there's a lot of coronavirus activity, close the bars, close the restaurants. That's heavy duty mitigation.

So I think with all of those things going on at the same time, I believe we will -- we're already doing it, but you just can't notice it yet because you have the dynamics of the virus going up. We're trying to put it down. You're not really sure quantitatively what you're doing, but you can be actually certain that we're having an impact on it.

As early as **March 20, 2020**, Ocean County police in Lakewood, New Jersey issued criminal charges to homeowner Eliyohu Zak for holding a 50-person wedding at his home. [68]

On **April 1, 2020**, at President Trump's intervention and direction, the U.S. Army Corps of Engineers finished constructing a 2,500 hospital bed, full-scale field hospital by converting the 1,800,000-square-foot Jacob K. Javits Convention Center in New York City. Because normal hospitals have more sophisticated, permanent equipment and capabilities

> The New York District of the Army Corps of Engineers has completed its conversion of the 1,800,000-square-foot Jacob K. Javits Convention Center in New York City into an alternate care facility for more than 2,000 non-COVID-19 patients.
>
> More than 165 New York District personnel provided design, engineering and construction support to facilitate the conversion in response to a Federal Emergency Management Agency request, said Michael Embrich, a Corps of Engineers spokesman.
>
> * * *
>
> "It was much quicker than we usually design, engineer and construct a project," he said. "We worked 24 hours a day, seven days a week with our vertical team to spec out the sites

[and] award contracts, and then began work immediately after the contracts were awarded."

Patients were able to move into the converted facility March 30, Embrich said.

The alternate care facility will not be used for COVID-19 patients. It will be used for non-COVID-19 patients, allowing area hospitals more room to treat patients infected by the coronavirus.

Contracts were recently awarded to convert additional locations in New York into alternate care facilities. Included among those are the Westchester County Community Center in White Plains, New York, and at the State University of New York's campuses at Stony Brook and Old Westbury on Long Island. Work should begin on those projects soon, Embrich said. [69]

On **April 6, 2020**, Trump authorized the use of the hospital ships for COVID-19 patients, which was not the original plan or their expertise: [70]

"If we need it for the virus, we will be using it for that," Trump said.

As of Monday, the *Comfort's* crew, which numbers roughly 1,200 people, had treated just 41 patients on the

1,000-bed vessel patients, according to the Defense Department. A total of 31 patients remain onboard, 16 of whom are in an intensive care unit.

Cuomo, speaking at a press conference, "as it turned out, there's not a lot of non-COVID people in the hospital system."

He attributed that to a decrease in the number of auto accidents and crime as a result of a city-wide lockdown on most businesses and social-distancing efforts by area residents.

"I'm going to call the president this afternoon and ask him to shift the Comfort from non-COVID to COVID," Cuomo said.

On **April 6, 2020**, New York Governor Andrew Cuomo, proclaimed that President Donald Trump has moved *"very quickly"* on responding to the COVID-19 threat and *"**has been helpful to New York in the past.**"*

"So I will call the President. He has been helpful to New York in the past. And he has moved very quickly in the past. I am going to ask if he can make this adjustment for us because it would be truly beneficial."

-- N.Y. Governor Andrew Cuomo, Press Conference, April 6, 2020, video from CNBC on You Tube, at time 12:18, *(emphasis added)* [71]

On **April 13, 2020**, [72] Governor Cuomo admitted that Donald Trump gave was very helpful to the State of New York in the COVID-19 crisis:

> "New York Gov. Andrew Cuomo is never shy to point out that President Donald Trump attacks him more than any other governor in America."

> "But on Monday, Cuomo took to an unlikely venue -- The Howard Stern Show -- to offer genuine praise for the president's response to the coronavirus in his home state."

> "'He has delivered for New York. He has,' Cuomo said of Trump, in response to a question from Stern about whether the president has really done anything of consequence to help.

> "'By and large it has worked,' Cuomo said of the relationship."

> "He cited, as he has before, the sending of the Navy ship USNS Comfort and the construction of a military field hospital at the Javits Center as examples of the president responding quickly to the state's needs."

> "He also, surprisingly, noted the president has even had a kind word for his brother Chris Cuomo - the CNN anchor who has himself been battling COVID-19...."

Life Long "Germophobe" President Warned the Nation Against New Virus: Updated October 2020:

But the level of dishonesty in our news media and our political world is breathtaking.

Their theme now is that Trump failed to warn the American people, and now he got what was coming to him, because he caught (and beat) the virus.

Mainstream journalists knew that Trump is a germophobe who warned the country, such as on February 26, 2020 in a press conference: [73]

> Washington (AFP) - Donald Trump had advice Wednesday for people worried by the coronavirus: be a germophobe like him.
>
> Frequent hand-washing has long been a quirk of the real estate billionaire and Republican president.
>
> He said his habit is exactly what's needed for protecting against the easily spread and potentially fatal coronavirus.
>
> "I do it a lot anyway as you probably heard," he told a press conference in the White House, triggering laughter.

In other words, Trump's excessive cleanliness to avoid catching a disease was so well-known in the news media and Washington, D.C., that the press corps chuckled at the reference and an anecdote

Trump shared. Similarly, *The Hill* also reported on Trump's warnings for the American people to treat the coronavirus like a germophobe like him:

> President Trump referenced his reputation as a germaphobe *[sic]* during a rare press conference about the coronavirus Wednesday.
>
> He suggested Americans take the same precautions they would during flu season, including avoiding unnecessary contact with public surfaces and people who are ill, as he always has.
>
> "I do it a lot anyway, as you've probably heard. Wash your hands. Stay clean. You don't have to necessarily grab every hand rail unless you have to," Trump said. "I mean, view this as the same as the flu. When somebody sneezes — I mean, I try to bail out as much as possible with the sneezing." [74]

From back in 2019 in *Politico*: [75]

> The president's admitted germaphobia *[sic]* has been a fixture throughout his career — from real-estate deal rooms to casino floors — and it's now popping up in more public ways. It could create another round of tactile challenges as Trump launches his 2020 campaign, during which he might try to steer visitors toward his

signature thumbs-up selfies and away from handshakes for the next 16 months.

He asks visitors if they'd like to wash their hands in a bathroom near the Oval Office. He'll send a military doctor to help an aide caught coughing on Air Force One

And the first thing he often tells his body man upon entering the Beast after shaking countless hands at campaign events: "Give me the stuff" — an immediate squirt of Purell.

Two and a half years into his term, President Donald Trump is solidifying his standing as the most germ-conscious man to ever lead the free world. His aversion shows up in meetings at the White House, on the campaign trail and at 30,000 feet.

Id.

The deceitful *New York Times* back on February 10, 2020, fear-mongered that Trump was so afraid of germs that he would be a dangerous national leader. They smeared Trump as over-reacting to the virus: [76]

WASHINGTON — When an outbreak of the Ebola virus touched the United States' shores in mid-2014, Donald J. Trump was still a private citizen. But he had strong opinions about how America should act.

Mr. Trump, who has spoken openly about his phobia of germs, closely followed the epidemic, and offered angry commentary about what he said was the Obama administration's dangerous response. He demanded draconian measures like canceling flights, forcing quarantines and even denying the return of American medical workers who had contracted the disease in Africa. [77]

* * *

Now Mr. Trump confronts another epidemic in the form of the coronavirus, this time at the head of the country's health care and national security agencies. The illness has infected few people in the United States, but health officials fear it could soon spread more widely. And while Mr. Trump has so far kept his distance from the issue, public health experts worry that his extreme fear of germs, disdain for scientific and bureaucratic expertise and suspicion of foreigners could be a dangerous mix, should he wind up overseeing a severe outbreak at home.

So on February 10, 2020, two weeks after Sen. Harris running for Vice President now says Trump should have known that the virus was a danger, "The Grey Lady," *The New York Times*, was fear-mongering that Trump was unfit to handle the virus.

Did President Trump Save Two Million Americans?

Trump was *too* afraid of germs, *too likely to over-react*, *too* prone to taking the virus *too seriously*.

But even while mocking Trump as over-reacting, *The New York Times* was forced to admit that:

> At the end of January, Mr. Trump created a 12-member coronavirus task force, which will be managed by the National Security Council. It includes the health and human services secretary, Alex M. Azar II; Dr. Anthony S. Fauci, the director of the National Institute of Allergy and Infectious Diseases at the National Institutes of Health; and Dr. Robert R. Redfield, the director of the Centers for Disease Control and Prevention.
>
> All three have experience dealing with infectious diseases, especially Mr. Fauci, who has helped to manage the response to numerous outbreaks, including the AIDS epidemic, the SARS virus and Ebola.

Id. And the dishonest *New York Times* gave away the store with:

> In his 2004 book, "How to Get Rich," the president declared himself "very much of a germophobe," and wrote that he was "waging a personal crusade to replace the mandatory and unsanitary handshake with the Japanese custom of bowing."

> As a result, Mr. Trump generally avoids the political tradition of shaking dozens of hands after his speeches and rallies, and frequently uses hand sanitizer. He is quick to banish aides who cough and sneeze in his presence. In a January 2017 interview, the president's personal physician, Dr. Harold N. Bornstein, said Mr. Trump always "changes the paper himself" in the examining room.

Id. So the idea that Trump was careless about the risks of the coronavirus are simply absurd lies. And the news media knows they are lying.

On January 27, 2020, as we will see, Trump tweeted to his 81 million tweeter followers that the Trump Administration was strongly watching the coronavirus. And he also established a coronavirus task force, announced on January 29.

On January 31, 2020, President Trump declared a national public health emergency.

And between January 17 and January 31, 2020, Trump shut down in stages all entry of travelers who had visited China or other virus hot spots within 14 days. (At the time, that was how long experts told us was needed for quarantine.)

Note that the ban was not on aircraft, but on travelers. It didn't matter where the aircraft was flying from. The ban was on people who had been in virus hot spots within 14 days, no matter what flight they were arriving on. So a person who changed flights in London could not enter. If a flight from Australia stopped in China for fuel, and no one got on, the aircraft could land in the U.S.A. But no traveler could enter who had been in an area with an outbreak. Note also that critics claim that the bureaucracy failed to fully and promptly implement Trump's orders. But the President ordered travel shut down. If his orders were disobeyed, that would be outrageous.

Was there some part of "*__EMERGENCY__*" that did not warn the American people? Isn't that the purpose, one purpose, of declaring an emergency?

And what part of the highly controversial shut down of travel from China – a huge news story – would not have alerted the American people that there was a danger and they needed to take the threat of the virus seriously?

During the debate among vice presidential candidates Kamala Harris and Mike Pence on October 7, 2020, Sen. Harris finally made the mistake of getting specific about the vague and foggy accusations against the Trump Administration.

Kamala Harris identified **January 28, 2020**, as the date when President Trump should have known that the coronavirus spreading from Wuhan, China, was a danger. And the attackers of Trump just lost their battle and their war right there. They can only level criticisms amid the fog of vagueness.

In fact, not only did President Donald J. Trump warn the American people openly and loudly and consistently to take precautions about the growing threat of a new coronavirus. But the depraved news media even mocked him for it in February.

DEMOCRAT-RUN NEW YORK CITY WAS THE INFERNO THAT FUELED EPIDEMIC NATION-WIDE

Special attention must be given to New York City, because the uncontrolled explosion in Democrat-ruled New York City and the States of New York and New Jersey, created a cauldron of an intense contagion and epidemic that spread from New York City to the rest of the United States.

The infection spread out nation-wide primarily from New York.[78] Democrat-run New York City was the furnace that drove the coronavirus epidemic throughout the rest of the entire United States.

So what went wrong? Unfortunately, the liberal, globalist, pro-immigration, anti-border policies of left-wing European nations allowed China's people fleeing the COVID-19 epidemic in Hubei Province, spreading throughout China, to run to Italy, Iran, Spain, etc. Because Europe is a border-less zone, COVID-19 spread quickly throughout Europe.

To be fair, most international travel from Europe lands at New York City's massive airports and much travel arrives at Newark, New Jersey. One of the most heavily-traveled corridors of airplane traffic is between London's Heathrow airport and New York City's John F. Kennedy International airport. The virus got into the country uncontrolled, not under quarantine restrictions, by a flood of travel from Europe. Of course, airplanes travel from China to Los Angeles, primarily, but Los Angeles did not experience much of a spread of the virus.

Because people come from Europe from so many original points of departure, and mingle within Europe, those infected could not be isolated and detected. Europe is a single European Union almost like a single country in terms of the ability of people to move freely anywhere within the continent.

But remember: President Trump has been trying to control our nation's borders. His critics are attacking him largely because they want uncontrolled borders with illegal aliens free to enter our country at will. Their positions would allow any pandemic to enter the country easily without restrictions. When Trump tried to control terrorism, his critics went nuts and ran to the courts.

And, yes, New York City is densely populated, but there are many other cities in the world that have high population density, such as Tokyo, Japan, and many Chinese cities. Yet Democrats who run New York City and New York State are supposed to know and understand the places they govern.

New York City's subway system jams commuters into cans like sardines, much closer than family members in their homes, breathing on one another within inches. Little was done to reduce the risk of the subway system.

Hotels starving for tourists could have housed nurses and medical support staff near their hospitals, reducing subway travel for essential employees. Same with major facilities like power plants, government, police stations, etc. RV's or mobile housing could have been set up in parking for those who could avoid travel home every day. Tourist buses thrown out of work could have been used to diversify travel on the streets above.

As late as **March 13, 2020**, Democrat DeBlasio believed that the virus could only be spread through bodily fluids – not through the air.[79]

Mayor DeBlasio kept New York's massive public school system [80] open[81] until **March 16, 2020** [82]

Mayor DeBlasio infamously urged New Yorkers on **March 2, 2020** [83] *to go out on the town to see a movie live* [84] *or a Broadway show*. [85]

On **February 2, 2020**, from the office of New York City's Health Commission, Commissioner Dave Chokshi encouraged New Yorkers to go out and enjoy the night life, explicitly including Chinese New Year. [86]

"As we gear up to celebrate the #LunarNewYear in NYC, I want to assure new Yorkers that there is no reason for anyone to change their holiday plans, avoid the subway, or

53

certain parts of the city because of #coronavirus."

Note that that China celebrated New Year around January 18 to 21, but New York's Chinese celebrated it in New York starting on January 25, but mainly culminating on February 9, 2020, with a massive parade and festival on that Sunday.[87]

Only two days later, Trump gave his State of the Union address **on February 4, 2020**, sternly warning and promising that the Trump Administration would take strong action to fight COVID-19.

On **February 2, 2020**, New York City's Commissioner of Health Oxiris Barbot encouraged New Yorkers to attend the parade on February 8, 2020, in a press conference carried on Fox News and elsewhere:

> "'The risk to new Yorkers from coronavirus is low and that our preparedness is very high. There is no reason not to take the subway, not to take the bus, not to go out to your favorite restaurant, and certainly not to miss the parade next Sunday. I am going to be there!'" [88]

January 24, 2020, New York City's Commissioner of Health Oxiris Barbot declared: [89]

> "New Yorkers should know the risk to residents of the city is low and that public health and emergency teams are ready to act swiftly if circumstances change."

NYC Mayor Bill DeBlasio resisted his own staff's demands to contain the virus. [90]

Democrat Governor Andrew Cuomo ordered active COVID-19 patients into nursing homes [91] despite Trump having an entire field hospital built for NYC that went unused and sending a hospital ship that went almost unused. Cuomo turned New York's nursing homes into incubators of the virus.

As even #NeverTrump CNN had to admit: [92]

> **Facts First:** Cuomo's assertion that "it never happened" is false. According to a report from the New York State Department of Health, "6,326 COVID-positive residents were admitted to [nursing home] facilities" following Cuomo's mandate that nursing homes accept the readmission of Covid-positive patients from hospitals. Whether or not this was "needed," it did in fact happen.

* * *

On March 25, the state's Health Department issued an advisory requiring nursing homes to accept "the expedited receipt of residents returning from hospitals" if the patients were deemed medically stable.

> "No resident shall be denied re-admission or admission to the [nursing home] solely based on a confirmed or suspected diagnosis of COVID-19," the advisory stated. "[Nursing homes] are prohibited from requiring a hospitalized resident who is

determined medically stable to be
tested for COVID-19 prior to
admission or readmission."

The report by the New York State Department of
Health analyzed the deadly blunder by Gov.
Cuomo. [93] The March 25, 2020, Advisory
ordering COVID-19 patients into New York nursing
homes can be downloaded here. [94]

Of course, the virus came from China.
Obviously, it is absurd to blame any country, ethnic
group or race just because a virus happened by
random chance to start in a particular region. But
the pragmatic reality is that those traveling to and
from China and with family and other relationships
with China would have – unfortunately and
regrettably – a higher probability of carrying the
virus from China to the New York City celebrations
of Chinese Lunar New Year. Disease can be cruel
and unfair, and we lament these circumstances.

We must grieve and pray for those in China
harmed by this act of nature, which is no fault of the
average Chinese people. There is nothing about
being Chinese, having Chinese ethnicity, or living
in China that *in any way* is responsible for this
virus. The average Chinese person is no more at
fault for COVID-19 than any family in Idaho or
Nebraska. We prayed for those in China and
applaud those Chinese Christian evangelists who
went to Hubei Province to pray for the sick and
encourage the people there.

When the Spanish Flu of 1918 killed an
estimated 50 million people (the world had just
emerged from World War I, so the world was in
chaos, making exact numbers difficult), no one
thought for one second that being Spanish had

anything to do with this flu pandemic. Don't be ridiculous. It was identified by its geographic point of origin (since disputed but assumed true at the time). If anyone thought that Spanish people were responsible, they were foolish. Back then, people had common sense. Nobody believed that the flu was caused, spread, or made worse in the slightest by the ethnic characteristics of Spanish people. Sadly, we don't have common sense any more.

But encouraging New Yorkers to join Chinese New Year when a virus was spreading from China (cruel as nature may be in that unfortunate circumstance) was a risk. Cold, hard, cruel math.

If a virus outbreak started in Nebraska, it would be common sense to limit contacts with Nebraska and people traveling to and from Nebraska. Yet, Democrats who run New York City encouraged precisely the opposite.

Only a few weeks later the same Lefitsts were screaming that everyone in the United States had to be locked down in their U.S. houses and not mingle with anyone at all.

There is a despicable effort to politicize a natural disaster and disease and blame President Trump as a cynical ploy to gain power.

Nevertheless, we must recall that the raging inferno of COVID-19 in New York City, affecting surrounding New York State and New Jersey, was the primary reason that the virus has spread throughout the rest of the country from New York and New Jersey, almost entirely from NYC.

WHEN SHOULD TRUMP HAVE STARTED ACTING?

The smears argue that Trump did not act quickly enough. But *starting from when*?

When was early? When was late? No one can measure "late," "early," or "on time," without first knowing when it became clear that there was a problem to respond to.

This is one of many major lies smearing Donald Trump. Most criticisms are intentionally vague about when an effective and responsible leader should have started responding.

Some say that the CDC warned of the virus on January 7, 2020. That is false. The CDC sent an alert on January 8, 2020, to physicians in the United States. The alert informed doctors that on January 5, 2020, China reported 59 (later revised downward to 41) cases of unexplained pneumonia.

The alert asked physicians to report if travelers from China returning to the USA exhibited any unusual symptoms or diseases. The January 8 alert indicated no threat to the United States and no epidemic in China either. The alert was a request for updates from physicians – not a warning of anything. It was a "be on the lookout" request gathering information, not offering any conclusions.

Only on **March 11, 2020**, did the World Health Organization finally declare[95] the COVID-19 coronavirus to be a worldwide pandemic. However, the Director-General also emphasized how unanticipated this development was:

"We have never before seen a pandemic sparked by a coronavirus.

This is the first pandemic caused by a coronavirus."

Two days later, Trump declared a national emergency on **March 13, 2020**. Two days later. Two days.

Note that Trump's January 31, 2020, "National Health Emergency" is different, under different laws, than a "National State of Emergency" which is more typically used for hurricanes, earthquakes, forest fires, tornadoes, etc. The January 31 declaration is more relevant and effective as being specific to the actual problem. The March 13 declaration just added a few more bullets to the artillery barrage against the virus already started in January. Again, a National Public Health Emergency (January 31) is very different from a National [Disaster] Emergency (March 13, 2020).

As late as **April 6, 2020**, ABC News reported that the Director of the CDC was "downplaying" the virus and explaining that "the death toll will be 'much lower' than projected." [96]

"'If we just social distance, we will see this virus and this outbreak basically decline, decline, decline. And I think that's what you're seeing,' said Robert Redfield, the Director of the Centers for Disease Control. "

"'I think you're going to see the numbers are, in fact, going to be much less than what would have been predicted by the models,' he said."

And ABC News also reported on **April 6, 2020**:

> "National Institute for Allergies and Infectious Disease Director Anthony Fauci said he was very interested in data in New York that the number of admissions to intensive care and intubations in the last three days had started to level off."

> "'We just got to realize that this is an indication despite all the suffering and the death that has occurred that what we have been doing has been working,'" he told reporters."

On **April 4, 2020**, two New York City Councilmen demanded that Mayor Bill DeBlasio fire New York City Commissioner of Health Oxiris Barbot because her guidance on COVID-19 had caused New York City not to prepare or respond and made the epidemic in New York State (centered in the city) much worse: [97]

> Two city lawmakers are demanding Mayor Bill de Blasio oust Health Commissioner Oxiris Barbot "before it's too late," saying her guidance on coronavirus has been disastrous.

> Barbot "failed to take decisive actions to not only contain the virus early and flatten the curve, but her inaction has actually led to New York City becoming the epicenter of this pandemic," City Councilmen Robert Holden and Eric Ulrich told de Blasio in a blistering letter obtained by The Post.

"Despite numerous warning signs from around the globe, Commissioner Barbot failed to keep New York City ahead of the curve. Significant research on pandemics and the spread of viruses should have been conducted early, and our city should have led the nation by taking drastic measures before any other city," it says.

As the global outbreak heated up in January, Barbot repeatedly assured New Yorkers their risk was "low," and to resume normal activities with only basic precautions such as washing hands.

On Feb. 2, with the city's first suspected coronavirus case under investigation and China's death toll skyrocketing, Barbot touted upcoming Chinese New Year events where crowds gather shoulder-to-shoulder in city streets.

"As we gear up to celebrate the #LunarNewYear in NYC, I want to assure New Yorkers that there is no reason for anyone to change their holiday plans, avoid the subway, or certain parts of the city because of #coronavirus," she tweeted.

Five days later, she declared the city had little to worry about. "We're telling New Yorkers, go about your lives, take the subway, go out, enjoy life," she said.

Barbot gave the city a false sense of security instead of tackling the harsh reality with aggressive measures, Holden told The Post.

"We should have taken more drastic steps early. Now we're paying the price in lives," he said.

* * *

"She's a self-proclaimed medical expert who got it terribly wrong," he said. "We're now facing the most devastating period in the outbreak. We need someone at the helm who is much more capable and competent to help us get through this. The mayor needs to find a new health commissioner — and he needs to do it fast, before it's too late."

On March 4, with COVID-19 cases emerging in Westchester County, Barbot dismissed the threat of infection by casual contact, saying, "There's no indication that being in a car, being in the subways with someone who's potentially sick is a risk factor," the letter notes.

At a City Hall press conference on March 5, with "only four confirmed cases" in NYC, Barbot said the city was urging people who arrived from certain countries with rising cases to self-isolate, but everybody else without symptoms should not have to quarantine.

No need for it," she said.

It's now widely accepted that COVID-19 can spread by people without symptoms, by casual contact, from touching virus-contaminated surfaces and through the air.

The councilmen blame Barbot for "irresponsible and reckless" inaction that helped spread the virus.

"She did not do enough to convince you to close public schools until March 16, and she failed to advise you to close playgrounds until Governor Andrew Cuomo made that decision for you," it says.

Remember: New York City was the epicenter, the inferno where the virus was spreading, the primary source from which it spread to the rest of the country from New York State and New Jersey. The assurances by NYC's leadership is not just one local city, but the place where the problem grew. New York City's mishandling of the virus is why the epidemic grew bad throughout the U.S.A.

As late as **March 9, 2020**, Dr. Anthony Fauci – who seems to be indignantly and with intense self-righteousness on both sides of every issue – encouraged people to go on cruise ship vacations [98] even after the disastrous experience of the *Diamond Princess* cruise ship, in which a couple thousand passengers were trapped in quarantine during a ship-board COVID-19 epidemic.

Speaking at a White House press conference tonight to provide updates on the COVID-19 Coronavirus situation, Dr. Anthony Fauci, director of the National Institute of Allergies and Infectious Diseases (NIAID), told reporters if you are healthy, there is no reason to eschew cruise vacations.

"If you are a healthy young person, there is no reason if you want to go on a cruise ship, go on a cruise ship."

Anthony Fauci, Director of NIAID

* * *

Fauci then said, "If you are a healthy young person, there is no reason if you want to go on a cruise ship, go on a cruise ship. But the fact is that if you have…an individual who has an underlying condition, particularly an elderly person who has an underlying condition, I would recommend strongly that they do not go on a cruise ship."

Vice President Mike Pence then followed up Fauci by saying advice to avoid vacations at sea was targeted to older people with "serious underlying conditions."

As late as **March 8, 2020**, there were only 550 cases of COVID-19 among the U.S.A's entire 331 million person population: [99]

> The number of confirmed U.S. cases of coronavirus reached nearly 550 on Sunday, including 22 deaths, according to state public health authorities and a running national tally kept by the Johns Hopkins University center tracking the outbreak.

Furthermore, on **March 8, 2020**, Dr. Anthony Fauci was only starting to suggest that the U.S. population might need to avoid crowds – but only "if the virus continued to spread."

> Fauci said authorities in the United States may also need to consider steps to keep people out of crowded places if the virus continued to spread. Still, he downplayed the likelihood of the type of large-scale mandatory quarantines imposed in China and Italy, while saying nothing could be ruled out.

Id.

On **March 5, 2020**, the New England Journal of Medicine first reported a case [100] in Germany of transmission of the infection from someone showing no symptoms. Only the first. March 5.

On **March 2, 2020**, New York City's Commissioner of Health Oxiris Barbot gave guidance to residents of New York City in a news conference broadcast on TV:

> "We know that there is currently no indication that it is easy to transmit by casual contact. There is no need to do any special anything in the community."

> "We want New Yorkers to go about their daily lives. Ride the subway. Take the bus. Go see your neighbors." [101]

On **March 2, 2020**, Democrat Mayor of New York City Bill DeBlasio, told New Yorkers in a press conference with Democrat New York Governor Mario Cuomo: [102]

> "'The facts are reassuring. All New Yorkers really should pay attention to this: We have a lot of information now. The information is actually showing us things that should give us more reason to stay calm and go about our daily lives.'"

The first cases of people becoming infected inside the United States were **February 26, 2020**, in California and Washington State [103] and in Virginia [104] and then **February 29, 2020**, in New Jersey.[105] So when should the Trump Administration have started taking action?

On **February 26, 2020**, it was big news that the first case was detected in California of a person who was apparently infected within the United States.[106] The woman was only the 60th COVID-19 case in the United States, according to *The New York Times* – as reported on February 26, 2020. *Id.*

> "A person in California who was not exposed to anyone known to be infected with the coronavirus and had not traveled to countries in which the virus is circulating, has tested positive for the infection. It may be the first case of community spread in the United States, the Centers for Disease Control and Prevention said on Wednesday." *Id.*

The New York Times further reported on **February 26, 2020**:

> "It brings the number of cases in the country to 60, including the 45 cases among Americans who were repatriated from Wuhan, China — the epicenter of the outbreak — and the Diamond Princess cruise ship, which was overwhelmed by the virus after it docked in Japan."

> "Until now, public health officials have been able to trace all of the infections in the country to a recent trip abroad or a known patient, and to identify the sources of exposure."

> "Though C.D.C. officials said it was possible the patient was exposed to a returning traveler who was infected,

the new case appears to be one of
community spread — one in which the
source of infection is unknown."

So, as late as **February 26, 2020**, all – all -- of
the 59 COVID-19 cases within the United States
were exclusively a result of U.S. citizens or lawful
permanent residents who were infected overseas in
foreign lands that were hot spots, and who returned
home to the U.S.A. The very first infection that
occurred within our country was only the 60th case
known in the entire nation of 331 million people.
And that was not until February 26, 2020.

On the same day, also **on February 26, 2020**,
the first death in the United States was reported. [107]
So the President would not have had much reason to
see a serious problem before the very first death
from the disease contracted inside the U.S. on
February 26, 2020, and only the second on
February 29, 2020.[108]

While these were not the first U.S. deaths from
COVID-19, all previous victims were infected
overseas where the virus was spreading, while
traveling in China or cooped up in cruise ships or
traveling through hot spots in Italy or Iran. Those
patients – U.S. citizens or lawful permanent
residents – were brought home and put into
quarantine and treated here in the United States. But
there was no evidence of the virus spreading inside
the United States. Isolated, transplanted people
infected overseas and returned home do not indicate
a problem with the disease spreading inside the
United States.

So the first time any prudent president would
have taken notice would be **February 29, 2020**,
when the second – only the second – person died

who was not infected overseas, but apparently (so far as we know) infected here on U.S. soil.

Prior to the second death of a U.S. citizen who did not catch the disease overseas, would a diligent, prudent, effective president have felt the need to take any unusual action? No, of course not.

There is a 45 minute video of a press conference on **February 25, 2020**, which is excellent and filled with great information and explanations. I am tempted to quote almost every part of the 45 minutes, and of course I cannot do that. Therefore, I would urge any interested person to carefully watch the press conference of The Department of Health and Human Services, especially in light of more recent controversies. One place it is visible is at on Facebook at https://www.facebook.com/watch/live/?extid=9sjV2 A9wXERQJmyt&v=569622150575091. [109]

Both Secretary Alex Azar and an expert announced in that event on **February 25, 2020**:

"The immediate risk to the American public remains low, but that has the potential to change quickly."

Azar starts out explaining that:

> "As of this morning *[February 25, 2020]*, we still have only 14 cases of the China coronavirus detected here in the United States involving travel to China or close contacts with those travelers. We have 3 cases among Americans repatriated from Wuhan. And we have 40 cases among American passengers who repatriated from the Diamond Princess *[cruise ship]* in Japan."

Finally, it was not until Wednesday, **February 25, 2020**, that the Centers for Disease control and Prevention, warned that an outbreak of the deadly virus in the United States is imminent. [110]

> "It's not so much a question of if this will happen anymore, but rather more a question of exactly when this will happen — and how many people in this country will have severe illness," said Dr. Nancy Messonnier, MD, the Director of the Center for the National Center for Immunization and Respiratory Diseases.

However, on **February 26, 2020**, there were only 60 cases (not deaths) in the entire United States of America of 331 million people: [111]

> A new case from California brings the total number infected in the U.S. to 60, most of them evacuated from outbreak zones.

Meanwhile on **February 26, 2020**, Virginia's Department of Health was publicly claiming that the ordinary influenza was a more serious threat than the new coronavirus:

> "Influenza virus, right now, is a much greater threat than any other coronavirus," said Dr. Scott Spillmann, with the Virginia Department of Health, in Danville. "For that reason, people should, if they

have not already gotten their flu shot yet, you have plenty of time to get it." *Id.*

On **February 27, 2020**, CDC Director Redfield testified before a U.S. House of Representatives Foreign Affairs subcommittee.[112]

He said: "It's important to note that this virus is not spreading within American communities at this time." *Id.*

Redfield testified that: "The potential global public health threat posed by this virus is high, but right now, the immediate risk to most Americans is low." And: "While community-wide transmission has not been documented yet in the United States, it is expected, and we are aggressively preparing for it."

On **February 17, 2020**, the CDC reaffirmed [113] that the "Based on current information, the risk from 2019-nCoV to the American public is currently deemed to be low. Nevertheless, CDC is taking proactive preparedness precaution."

As late as **February 15, 2020**, in Europe, only the very first death was confirmed on the entire European continent. The very first death in Europe was infected back home in China, and fled to France, probably to run from the epidemic in China, as the BBC News reported: [114]

"A Chinese tourist has died in France after contracting the new coronavirus - the first fatality from the disease outside Asia. The victim was an 80-year-old man from China's Hubei

71

province, according to French Health Minister Agnès Buzyn. He arrived in France on 16 January and was placed in quarantine in hospital in Paris on 25 January, she said. Only three deaths had previously been reported outside mainland China - in Hong Kong, the Philippines and Japan.

Furthermore, the BBC News reported that Director General Tedros Adhanom Ghebreyesus said worldwide "relatively little" was spent on preparedness for a virus outbreak, he said, compared with preparations for a possible terrorist attack. The lack of preparedness was in all countries, not allegedly in the United States.

Therefore, as late as **February 15, 2020**, there were ZERO (0) deaths in Europe (as far as we knew at the time) of anyone who became infected within the vast borders of Europe. The very first death was a victim infected in China who traveled to Europe.

On **February 14, 2020**, the Coronavirus, Democrat New York City Mayor De Blasio said February 14th," should not stop you from going about your life, should not stop you from going to Chinatown and going out to eat. I'm going to do that today myself." [115]

It was not until **February 10, 2020**, that *inside China itself*, deaths from COVID-19 exceeded deaths inside China from the SARS outbreak 17 years earlier. Inside China where the COVID-19 pandemic began, there were "908 reported deaths in China in the last month compared with 774 deaths in the SARS crisis." [116]

On **February 7, 2020**, New York City's Commissioner of Health Oxiris Barbot gave guidance to residents of New York City on TV news channel 'Spectrum New York 1': [117]

> "[Oxiris Barbot] 'The important thing for New Yorkers to know is that in the city currently their risk is low, and our city preparedness is high. And so we know that this virus can be transmitted from one individual to another, but that it's typically people who live together. That there's no risk at this point in time — we're always learning more — about having it be transmitted in casual contact.' '"

> "[Oxiris Barbot] ''Right? So we're telling New Yorkers, go about your lives, take the subway, go out, enjoy life, but practice everyday precautions,' she said.

Tom Elliott
@tomselliott

NYC "Health Commissioner" Oxiris Barbot on Feb. 7th: "We're telling New Yorkers, go about your lives, take the subway, go out, enjoy life"

NEWS

DR. OXIRIS BARBOT
CITY HEALTH COMMISSIONER

10:03 AM · Mar 27, 2020

♡ 4.3K   ♡ 3.9K people are Tweeting about this

Again, New York and New Jersey were the inferno that fed the virus to the rest of the U.S.A.

> "[Question from news anchor] 'Right so we don't know if it can be transmitted by casual contact, but we don't know what kind of contact is required, right?'"

> "[Oxiris Barbot] 'Well, we know that it can be transmitted when people are living together and have extended contact. We also know that if it were likely to be transmitted casually, we would be seeing a lot more cases." "

> "[Question from news anchor] 'Right, right. Because this is New York and you are in elevators and trains with everybody all the time.'"

> "[Oxiris Barbot] 'Exactly.'"

On **February 5, 2020**, the CDC issued a public statement saying, [118] **"We continue to believe the immediate risk of coronavirus exposure to the general public is low**, however, CDC is undertaking these measures to help keep that risk low."

On **February 5, 2020**, Senator Chuck Schumer (D-NY) accused on Twitter: [119]

> "The premature travel ban to and from China by the current administration is just an excuse to his on-going war against immigrants."

Joe Biden attacked Trump in February for Trump's racist and xenophobic over-reaction.

Joe Biden ✓
@JoeBiden

Stop the xenophobic fear-mongering. Be honest. Take responsibility. Do your job.

> **Donald J. Trump** ✓ @realDonaldTrump · Mar 18
> I always treated the Chinese Virus very seriously, and have done a very good job from the beginning, including my very early decision to close the "borders" from China - against the wishes of almost all. Many lives were saved. The Fake News new narrative is disgraceful & false!

3:35 PM · Mar 18, 2020 · Twitter Web App

On **January 31, 2020**, the day the travel ban was announced, Joe Biden called it "hysterical xenophobia and fear-mongering." [120]

> "The American people need to have a president who they can trust what he says about it, that he is going to act rationally about it. In moments like this, this is where the credibility of the president is most needed as he explains what we should and should not do. This is no time for Donald Trump's record of hysteria xenophobia — hysterical xenophobia and fear-mongering."

When Americans began practicing "social distancing," Congresswoman Alexandria Ocasio-Cortez (D-N.Y.) accused them of racism.

> "Honestly, it sounds almost so silly to say, but there's a lot of restaurants that are feeling the pain of racism, where people are literally not

> patroning [sic] Chinese   restaurants,
> they're   not   patroning [sic]   Asian
> restaurants because of just straight up
> racism around the Coronavirus," she
> said on Instagram Live. [121]

Democratic colleague, Rep. Ayanna Pressley (D-Mass.) likewise accused Americans of being "racist" for practicing what are now widely accepted as the best practices to prevent Coronavirus' spread.

> "'You know, since the beginning of
> the COVID-19 outbreak, we've seen
> not only the spreading of the virus but
> also a rapid spreading of racism and
> xenophobia,' the lawmaker said
> during a congressional oversight
> hearing. 'We have witnessed it at the
> highest levels and, in fact, the
> Republican Party fanning,
> irresponsibly, these flames. One
> colleague tweeted that, 'Everything
> you need to know about the Chinese
> Coronavirus.' My district is home to
> nearly 32 percent foreign-born
> residents, with more than a quarter
> immigrating from Asia. This painful
> rhetoric has consequences.
> Restaurants across Boston's
> Chinatown have seen up to an 80%
> drop in business. And I believe this
> has everything to do with the rapid
> spread of misinformation and
> paranoia.'" [122]

News Grabien reminds us back on memory lane, including with a video montage on AirTV at https://www.air.tv/?v=KgXbxTw5TnydP4xVuoC3r A [123]

> "Americans, and Trump, were likewise attacked in the media. On CNN, contributor Jeff Yang said Americans were being racist for avoiding crowds and especially those sneezing and coughing."

> "'A lot of Asian-Americans and Asians in other countries, who are experiencing I guess you could say a metaphorically cold shoulder when it comes to being in public and simply being, you know, Chinese in a crowded space,' Yang said." It's something that causes people to part like the red sea, daring to cough or sneeze causes people to actually shy away from you. There is a sense in which people feel very much like there's a kind of racial profiling occurring, simply because the disease so is far has been primarily limited in terms of fatalities.'" [124]

Of course, U.S. citizens and lawful permanent residents – of all ethnicities of course -- had a right to come home. They were put through medical screening and placed in quarantine as required. We were going to leave U.S. citizens stranded overseas? The delays in returning cruise ship passengers [125] were huge scandals already in the nightly news. [126]

On **February 3, 2020**, as Bloomberg reported: "China Blasts U.S. for 'Overreaction' to Virus, Spreading Fear." [127]

On **January 30, 2020**, Director Robert R. Redfeld of the Centers for Disease Control announced [128] testified that

> "We understand that this may be concerning, but based on what we know now, we still believe the immediate risk to the American people is low."

On **January 30, 2020**, the CDC confirmed publicly for the first time [129] that the virus had spread person-to-person, which the W.H.O. and China had previously denied, in the United States. The CDC also declared that by January 30 "NIAID has responded to public health concerns about COVID-19 by increasing ongoing coronavirus research efforts to accelerate the development of interventions that could help control current and future outbreaks of COVID-19."

It was not until **January 30, 2020**, that the World Health Organization declared the outbreak of the then-new coronavirus to be a "global health emergency." [130]

On **January 29, 2020**, experts were saying Trump was over-reacting. For example, Marc Siegel, M.D. wrote in the *Los Angeles Times*, "Wuhan Coronavirus is not a threat, but the Flu is." [131]

On **January 26, 2020**, NIH Director Dr. Anthony Fauci said according to The Hill, [132] "the American public shouldn't worry about the coronavirus outbreak in China. "It's a very, very low risk to the United States," Fauci said this during an interview with radio show host John Catsimatidis on WABC.

On **January 23, 2020**, at an emergency committee convened by the World Health Organization, [133] the W.H.O. announced that the Wuhan coronavirus does not yet constitute a public health emergency of international concern.

On **January 21, 2020**, Washington State's government Secretary of Health John Wiesman explained "**We believe the risk to the public is low.**" [134]

JANUARY 21, 2020 -- "We believe the risk to the public is low," added Washington State Secretary of Health John Wiesman.

On **January 21, 2020**, during a television interview with NewsMax TV host Greg Kelly, Fauci said of the coronavirus:

> "Obviously, you need to take it seriously, and do the kinds of things that the CDC and the Department of Homeland Security are doing. But this is not a major threat for the people of the United States, and this is not something that the citizens of the United States right now should be worried about." [135]

It was not until **January 21, 2020**, when the World Health Organization did not acknowledge that the coronavirus could spread from human to human (as opposed to consuming a common source of contaminated food for example).

On **January 21, 2020**, Zhong Nanshan, MD, a prominent Chinese scientist, confirmed that the mysterious coronavirus that has killed at least 4 people and infected more than 200 in China is capable of being transmitted from person to person, according to *The New York Times*. [136]

On **January 21, 2020**, [137]

> "At this point, the World Health Organization (WHO) still has doubts about the roots of what would become the COVID-19 pandemic, noting that the spate of pneumonia-like cases in Wuhan could have stemmed from a new coronavirus. There are 59 cases so far, and travel precautions are already at the forefront of experts' concerns."

China, as late as **January 20, 2020**, was holding their gigantic, nation-wide celebrations of New Year's with massive crowds, parties, parades, and gatherings. China, where the virus started, was acting like nothing was wrong, at the epicenter of the pandemic.

Shortly after the end of the New Years' celebrations, suddenly China went into lockdowns and quarantines in the City of Wuhan and its surrounding Hubei Province. But that was not until after January 21, 2020.

Inside, China, government behavior switched suddenly while China only a small number of deaths: [138]

> "In just 2 days, 13 more people died and an additional 300 were sickened. China makes the unprecedented move not only to close

off Wuhan and its population of 11 million, but to also place a restricted access protocol on Huanggang, 30 miles to the east, where residents can't leave without special permission. This means up to 18 million people are under strict lockdown."

On **January 20, 2020**, the Centers for Disease Control and Prevention ordered screening for coronavirus to begin at three (3) US Airports, while also directing travellers inbound to the United States from China or the region of China to be diverted to those airports.

Three additional cases of what is now the 2019 novel coronavirus are reported in Thailand and Japan, causing the CDC to begin screenings at JFK International, San Francisco International, and Los Angeles International airports. These airports are picked because flights between Wuhan and the United States bring most passengers through them.

The CDC announced on **January 17, 2020**, "based on current information, the risk from 2019-nCoV to the American public is currently deemed to be low." [139]

On **January 14, 2020**, the World Health Organization announced: [140]

"@WHO Preliminary investigations conducted by the Chinese authorities have found no clear evidence of human-to-human transmission of the

> novel   #coronavirus   (2019-nCoV)
> identified in #Wuhan, #China. "

On January 10, 2020, The New York Times reported the first – only the first -- death from COVID-19 in China. [141]

> Chinese state media on Saturday reported the first known death from a new virus that has infected dozens of people in China and set off worries across Asia.
>
> The Xinhua news agency cited the health commission in the central Chinese city of Wuhan, where the illness first appeared, in reporting the death. The health commission said the patient, a 61-year-old man, died on Thursday night.
>
> Forty-one people have been found to have the new virus, a coronavirus, and seven patients are still in severe condition, the health commission said, according to the Xinhua report. Two patients have been discharged, it said.
>
> There is no evidence that the virus can be spread between humans, according to the commission. The initial cases were linked to workers at a market that sold live fish, birds and other animals. More than 700 people who had close contact with patients, including 419 medical workers, have been put under observation, the

commission said, adding that no additional cases have been found.

As of **January 8, 2020**, information was still vague, useless, and uncertain. Note the key claims "believe" and "may be" – don't know:

> "The World Health Organization confirmed on Wednesday that Chinese authorities believe a new coronavirus — from the family that produced SARS and MERS — may be the cause of mysterious pneumonia cases in the city of Wuhan."

> "The Chinese government has not yet publicly stated that a coronavirus is the cause of the illness, which has infected at least 59 people. But the Wall Street Journal reported that was the case earlier Wednesday, citing unnamed sources."

> "'Coronaviruses are a large family of viruses that range from the common cold to SARS. Some cause less-severe disease, some more severe. Some transmit easily from person to person, while others don't,' the WHO statement said."

> "The virus can cause severe illness in some patients, the agency said, adding that it does not "transmit readily" between people. Earlier statements from the Wuhan Municipal Health Authority said there has been no

person-to-person spread — a claim disease experts say is impossible to make at this stage in the exploration of a new disease. " [142]

Notice the key information as of January 8, 2020: "The virus can cause severe illness in some patients, the agency said, adding that **it does not 'transmit readily' between people."**

So elected national leaders around the world and public health officials were informed officially by China and the World Health Organization that it was *difficult* to catch the virus from another person. If you were a government decision maker and you were told by the W.H.O. that the virus *does not "transmit readily" between people* how would that affect governmental decision-making?

Back on **January 8, 2020**, the CDC issued a Health Alert Network advisory [143] notifying health care providers to ask patients in the United States about recent travel in China. The alert advised that "as of January 5, 2020, the national authorities in China have reported 59 patients with [Pneumonia of Unknown Etiology] to W.H.O." It explained that "Wuhan City is a major transportation hub about 700 miles south of Beijing with a population of more than 11 million people."

So as of **January 5, 2020**, *only* 59 suspicious pneumonia patients were reported in China – *none in the U.S.* And yet the CDC was already asking doctors to be on the lookout for unexplained pneumonia in the United States and/or patients who had recently visited China. Critics smearing Trump say that Trump was warned by the CDC on January 7, 2020. That is a lie. The CDC warned doctors that in China, not in the U.S., there were only 59 cases.

(Of course China was itself lying, but no one knew that then back here.)

Some claim that intelligence agencies warned of the pandemic in November or December. On April 8, 2020, ABC News dropped a bombshell. "Intelligence report warned of coronavirus crisis as early as November: Sources: 'Analysts concluded it could be a cataclysmic event, a source said.' "

> As far back as late November, U.S. intelligence officials were warning that a contagion was sweeping through China's Wuhan region, changing the patterns of life and business and posing a threat to the population, according to four sources briefed on the secret reporting.

> Concerns about what is now known to be the novel coronavirus pandemic were detailed in a November intelligence report by the military's National Center for Medical Intelligence (NCMI), according to two officials familiar with the document's contents.

> The report was the result of analysis of wire and computer intercepts, coupled with satellite images. It raised alarms because an out-of-control disease would pose a serious threat to U.S. forces in Asia -- forces that depend on the NCMI's work. And it paints a picture of an American government that could have ramped up mitigation

and containment efforts far earlier to prepare for a crisis poised to come home.

"Analysts concluded it could be a cataclysmic event," one of the sources said of the NCMI's report. "It was then briefed multiple times to" the Defense Intelligence Agency, the Pentagon's Joint Staff and the White House. Wednesday night, the Pentagon issued a statement denying the "product/assessment" existed. [144]

Notice how the "two officials familiar with the document's contents" are anonymous sources. They did not go on the record and they are not named.

Small problem. The ABC News report was totally false. The National Center for Medical Intelligence was so adamant that the ABC report was false that it broke its normal secrecy and normal refusal to comment: [145]

"'As a matter of practice, the National Center for Medical Intelligence does not comment publicly on specific intelligence matters,' Day said. 'However, in the interest of transparency during this current public health crisis, we can confirm that media reporting about the existence/release of a National Center for Medical Intelligence Coronavirus-related product/assessment in November of 2019 is not correct. No such NCMI product exists.'" [146]

Even the Trump haters in Congress who want to investigate everything dropped the topic like a hot potato. There was never any truth to it. Yet this falsehood is still argued in social media by angry Leftists.

So a diligent, prudent president would not have started to take strong action until around February 29, 2020. Again, the evidence shows a transitional period from February 25, 2020, through March 11, 2020, when the experts were still reassuring the public, but starting to change their tune. So the tide was indecisive and choppy (if you have seen the tide change directions in a harbor or inlet) from February 25 to March 11. No President could be blamed for any lack of action before March 11.

THE WORLD HEALTH ORGANIZATION SAID DON'T WORRY ABOUT IT

The World Health organization got most things wrong at every stage of this pandemic. No one can under-estimate the significance of this on the actions of governments around the world.

The W.H.O. told decision-makers all around the world on January 14, 2020, that the virus that causes COVID-19 is not spread from person to person (there is no evidence that it spreads from one person to another). [147]

This is a galaxy sized blunder that caused massively bad decision-making in every country in the world. All of the nation's leaders and public health officials were officially led to believe that COVID-19 was not contagious in the traditional sense of spreading from one person to another as is the flu such as by coughing.

Sure, everyone makes mistakes. You can shrug it off as "the fog of war" so to speak. But no. This was guidance to the entire world from the supposed world authority on public health issues *not* to prepare for a contagious disease, informing the world's national leaders and public health professionals that COVID-19 was *not* contagious and would not spread from person to person. Yes, W.H.O. said "no evidence" but what was the purpose and effect of saying this at all? Do *not* start stockpiling supplies. Do *not* gear up for an epidemic or international pandemic. Do *not* start preparing hospital capacity. Do *not* start activating teams to respond to the threat.

In short, don't worry about it. "What, me worry?"[148]

W.H.O.'s announcement was effectively a *stand down" order* – as late as January 14, 2020. Stand down. There is no contagious disease threat. The virus will not spread from one person to another.

And what makes this so significant is that W.H.O. has a uniquely tight relationship with China. Some say W.H.O. is in China's back pocket. And China was blocking everyone else from information about the disease. W.H.O. and China had a monopoly on details about the new coronavirus spreading in China's Hubei Province. So when W.H.O. spoke, they spoke as about the only organization with actual knowledge.

We can shrug this off as a minor thing, but it is gigantic. At a crucial, early stage of the pandemic, the world's supposed expert organization pointed completely in the wrong direction. If you want to blame anyone, W.H.O's massive mistake caused every nation on the Earth to not prepare for the pandemic and to think about it in completely wrong ways. However, the Trump Administration did not completely believe W.H.O. and investigated on its own – despite intense Chinese resistance and mis-direction.

We're not sure what the W.H.O. had in mind and was trying to say. Clearly, COVID-19 was in fact spreading from human to human within Hubei Province in China and its provincial capital of Wuhan. Since the virus was rapidly spreading in China, we can only guess what other methods of transmission the W.H.O. was thinking about.

There can be other ways in which disease can spread, such as being bitten by mosquitos carrying malaria, deer ticks carrying Lyme's Disease or fleas carrying some diseases. A disease can spread from a common source. Supposedly, "Legionnaire's Disease" might have spread to large gatherings (originally a convention) from a common infection in the air conditioning system of a building, so that the disease did not spread person to person. It spread to people sharing a building from a common source in the building. Perhaps the disease could have spread from drinking from the same contaminated water, eating the same contaminated food supply, sexual activity, drinking from the same glasses or using the same knife, forks, spoons, etc.

But we don't know what W.H.O. was thinking as an alternative to "human to human transmission." Clearly W.H.O.'s signal to the world's decision-makers was that there is no danger of contagion in the human population.

I am not aware that W.H.O. ever offered any other explanation other than the unsubstantiated rumors of people eating infected bats from the

Wuhan Seafood market. No one ever found such a bat. The type of bats suspected of being likely to carry coronaviruses are found hundreds of miles away and don't live around Wuhan. This idea of people eating bats was a total guess.

There are witnesses that there were no bats sold at the Wuhan Seafood market. A Lancet paper published on February 15, 2020, by physicians who treated some of the first COVID-19 patients in China showed that "Patient Zero" -- the one believed to have started the transmission, was nowhere near the Wuhan seafood market.

> "The very first patient identified had *not* been exposed to the market, suggesting the virus may have originated elsewhere and been transported to the market, where it was able to thrive or jump from human to animal and back again." [149] [150]

Similarly, the world's public health agencies and officials and medical professionals made a severe, different, but related mistake: As described by at least one medical expert to STAT News serving the medical community, researchers got stuck on a critical, but wrong, assumption. They saw signs that indicated that the coronavirus was behaving differently outside of China than the rapid spread that had swept through Hubei Province and that region. This caused a delay in responding and questions that ate up valuable time. [151]

> "Yes, there were cases outside China — just over 100 had been reported to the World Health Organization by Jan.

31 — but they were spread out in relatively small numbers in 19 countries. The virus, the thinking went, didn't appear to be behaving as explosively outside of China as it had inside it."

"In hindsight, that argument, from a biological point of view, didn't make any sense — and it ignored a soon-to-be-apparent Epidemiology 101 lesson: It takes time for a virus that spreads from person to person to hit an exponential growth phase in transmission, even if every new case was infecting on average two to three other people."

"It wasn't that the virus was behaving differently; we simply hadn't yet seen what it was doing as it moved beyond China. When large outbreaks exploded in Iran and then Northern Italy in late February, the reality became abundantly evident. And then it was too late."

"'Everybody was in denial of this coming, including the U.S. And everybody got hit — just as simple as that,' Gary Kobinger, director of the Infectious Disease Research Center at Laval University in Quebec, told STAT."

It is your author's opinion, but I think the analysis has to consider the confusion generated by

W.H.O.'s guidance that the virus might not be spread human-to-human like a typical contagious infection. That diversion and incorrect information probably made people stop and hesitate when they normally would not have doubted their training and common sense.

If the virus was spreading in China by some other mechanism than being carried by breath like the flu, then the virus might actually spread through Middle Eastern and European populations differently. That is, if some mechanism was distributing the virus in China, which was not happening elsewhere, in addition to more typical transmission like the flu through breathing, coughing, sneezing, contaminated surfaces, etc. , then the transmission might be much slower in Europe, Iran, etc. But that idea was a serious mistake.

TRUMP SAVED TWO MILLION LIVES

I believe you will be convinced by the end of this book. The strong, effective leadership of President Donald Trump saved 2 million Americans. Let's delve into this in detail throughout the course of this book.

The experts' models projected [152] that 2.2 million U.S. citizens and residents would die[153] from COVID-19. [154] Leftists adore and worship experts. So let's assume for the sake of comparison that these predictions are correct.

Were those predictions correct? Well they are all we have to go by. In terms of what would have happened without Trump's leadership, the estimates that Trump's critics believe in and argue from are the only measure we have of the difference between no action and Trump's actions and leadership responding to the pandemic.

If we are going to counter the attacks and distortions, we do need to compare apples to apples and oranges to oranges, as the saying goes.

So whether you buy this reasoning or not, Trump's critics do. So we have to respond to their criticism on the same terms that they argue, at least in part.

Trump's critics attack the President for – they claim – not acting soon enough and effectively. Why didn't the President (any president) wave his magic wand and stop the virus? Isn't there a secret button in the Oval Office or something?

That is essentially what Trump's critics are fervently, vigorously, loudly, arguing now over and over again. Democrats insist that anything that goes wrong is automatically Trump's fault. A virus killed people. Therefore, Trump is to blame.

Trump should have used *magic* to stop the virus.

So if we are going to analyze and respond to the criticisms, let's start with the same framework and way of thinking and premises that we are responding to. Rather than being like ships passing in the night, let's meet the criticisms head on. We must use their type of arguments to respond to their attacks.

One of many studies that got the most attention was from Imperial College of London, in a team led by Neil Ferguson. [155] On pages 6-7 of this March 16, 2020, report [156]

by the "Imperial College COVID-19 Response Team," they state the conclusion:

"Results"

"In the (unlikely) absence of any control measures or spontaneous changes in individual behaviour, [157] we would expect a peak in mortality (daily deaths) to occur after approximately 3 months (Figure 1A). In such scenarios, given an estimated R0 of 2.4, we predict 81% of the GB and US populations would be infected over the course of the epidemic. Epidemic timings are approximate given the limitations of surveillance data in both countries: The epidemic is predicted to be broader in the US than in GB and to peak slightly later. This is due to the larger geographic scale of the US, resulting in more distinct localised epidemics across states (Figure 1B) than seen across GB. The higher peak in mortality in GB is due to the smaller size of the country and its older population compared with the US. In total, in an unmitigated epidemic, we would predict approximately 510,000 deaths in GB and 2.2 million in the US, not accounting for the potential negative effects of health systems being overwhelmed on mortality.

So, at least 2.2 million people would have died in the United States, had Trump not taken all the actions that he did, directly and through his Administration. Note that the projected deaths could have soared higher than 2.2 million due to "the potential negative effects of health systems being overwhelmed on mortality" they projected. That is, if the hospitals and medical system were overwhelmed with the quantity of patients, the number of deaths would likely be even worse.

As late as May 4, 2020, experts were predicting that there would be 3,000 deaths per day -- that would be 90,000 almost 100,000 deaths per month: "A draft government report projects Covid-19 cases will surge to about 200,000 per day by June 1, a staggering jump that would be accompanied by more than 3,000 deaths each day." [158] The report was presented by the Centers for Disease Control and Prevention. [159]

But President Trump's leadership brought those projected deaths down to 214,081 (as of this writing in early September).[160]

So Trump's leadership saved the lives of 2 million Americans.

It's simple: 2.2 million deaths were projected in the United States by medical experts – 214,081 actual deaths as of this writing = a saving of 2 million people who did not die. Two million people

Yes, that is the correct measure. The projection of 2.2 million deaths was based on the assumption that the U.S. Government did *not* take actions to control the disease.

But Trump did! So the projection of 2.2 million deaths changed to only 214,081 deaths because of what the Trump Administration actually did.

Leftists will sputter that this is not the correct analysis. But they are wrong. Yes, this is the correct analysis. 2.2 million dead without effective national leadership. Only 214,081 as of early September after measures taken by the Trump Administration and the States under his leadership.

Leftists attempt to argue "Oh, no, the 2.2 million number of dead was if we did not take action." Uhhh.... *Yeah...* that's exactly the analysis. Trump *did* take action. That's the whole point. *Absolutely!*

In fact, the Imperial College report discussed the tremendous complexity and challenges of managing this problem in all its many details and variables, on page 14:

"Discussion"

"As the COVID-19 pandemic progresses, countries are increasingly implementing a broad range of responses. Our results demonstrate that it will be necessary to layer multiple interventions, regardless of whether suppression or mitigation is the overarching policy goal. However, suppression will require the layering of more intensive and socially disruptive measures than mitigation. The choice of interventions ultimately depends on the relative feasibility of their implementation and their likely effectiveness in different social contexts."

"Disentangling the relative effectiveness of different interventions from the experience of countries to date is challenging because many have implemented multiple (or all) of these measures with varying degrees of success. Through the hospitalisation of all cases (not just those requiring hospital care), China in effect initiated a form of case isolation, reducing onward transmission from cases in the household and in other settings. At the same time, by implementing population-wide social distancing, the opportunity for onward transmission in all locations was rapidly reduced. Several studies have estimated that these interventions reduced R to below 1. 15 In recent days, these measures have begun to be relaxed. Close monitoring of the situation in China in the coming weeks will therefore help to inform strategies in other countries."

So this is really complicated. Every action has inter-connected, inter-related, overlapping impacts. Deciding what to do requires seeing all the inter-relationships. The difficulty, challenges, and complexity for national leaders managing this problem is further explained on page 15:

> "However, there are very large uncertainties around the transmission of this virus, the likely effectiveness of different policies and the extent to which the population spontaneously adopts risk reducing behaviours. This means it is difficult to be definitive about the likely initial duration of measures which will be required, except that it will be several months. Future decisions on when and for how long to relax policies will need to be informed by ongoing surveillance.

> "The measures used to achieve suppression might also evolve over time."

And on pages 7-8, the Imperial College report went on to say:

> "For an uncontrolled epidemic, we predict critical care bed capacity would be exceeded as early as the second week in April, with an eventual peak in ICU or critical care bed demand that is over 30 times greater than the maximum supply in both countries (Figure 2). The aim of mitigation is to reduce the impact of

an epidemic by flattening the curve, reducing peak incidence and overall deaths (Figure 2). Since the aim of mitigation is to minimise mortality, the interventions need to remain in place for as much of the epidemic period as possible. Introducing such interventions too early risks allowing transmission to return once they are lifted (if insufficient herd immunity has developed); it is therefore necessary to balance the timing of introduction with the scale of disruption imposed and the likely period over which the interventions can be maintained. In this scenario, interventions can limit transmission to the extent that little herd immunity is acquired – leading to the possibility that a second wave of infection is seen once interventions are lifted."

In other words, one major purpose of the interventions is to slow the *velocity* of the infectious disease so that the volume / quantity does not exceed the maximum capabilities of the hospital systems and medical abilities of our nation.

But Trump's leadership did not cause deaths but prevented around 2 million projected deaths.

It is interesting to read that the Imperial College report also explains on page 4:

"We do not consider the ethical or economic implications of either strategy here, except to note that there is no easy policy decision to be made.

Suppression, while successful to date in China and South Korea, carries with it enormous social and economic costs which may themselves have significant impact on health and well-being in the short and longer-term. Mitigation will never be able to completely protect those at risk from severe disease or death and the resulting mortality may therefore still be high. Instead we focus on feasibility, with a specific focus on what the likely healthcare system impact of the two approaches would be. We present results for Great Britain (GB) and the United States (US), but they are equally applicable to most high-income countries."

It is worth reading the Imperial College report, even though you may not agree with it. There are many passages of interest.

NO, TRUMP NEVER SAID THE VIRUS IS A HOAX

Unfortunately, there is a growing part of American society that is willing to tell any lie to gain power or gain advantage. Lying has become as normal as breathing for too many who want to take control over your life and accumulate power.

Trump never said that the coronavirus is or was a hoax. That's a knowing lie.

On February 4, 2020, in his state of the union address, [161] Trump showed that he took the disease very seriously and explained how he was already taking action:

> Protecting Americans' health also means fighting infectious diseases. We are coordinating with the Chinese government and working closely together on the coronavirus outbreak in China. My administration will take all necessary steps to safeguard our citizens from this threat.

But during a February 28, 2020, campaign rally in South Carolina,[162] Trump criticized Democrats for turning the virus into "their new hoax." Trump haters then attacked Trump for calling the virus a hoax and not taking it seriously.

But Trump addressed the epidemic on February 4, 2020, in his national State of the Union address.

Trump could not have meant that the hoax was the virus, when he called fighting it a priority 24 days earlier. It is his Democrat opponents lying about him whom he called a hoax.

And they are still lying about Trump today. This briefing documents the hoax of Democrat and anti-Trump Republican propaganda.

Imagine, if you will a Twilight Zone in which Donald Trump warns that the Democrats are creating a "hoax" lying about Trump's handling of the COVID-19 threat, and Democrats then turn Trump's warning into an accusation that Trump is not taking the viral pandemic seriously.

Got that? The Democrats are actually doing even up to this moment exactly what Trump warned they were doing: Lying about Trump's response to the COVID-19 crisis. Democrat lies are the hoax.

Other than _World Net Daily_ and _Daily Wire_, I am not aware of any credible or reliable "fact check" outfits. Do you know who these so-called "fact checkers" are? Do you know if they are biased? Should we believe them?

SNOPES is not a news source. But when the Left-wing couple who started SNOPES in their basement with their cat (as they proudly showed themselves), defends Donald Trump, you have to stand up in shock and take notice.

When Snopes says that Left-wing attacks on any Republican are not true, heaven gasps in astonishment, the stars stop and shudder for a moment, and the galaxy stops spinning for a split second to recover from the amazement.

Well, here is what even SNOPES had to admit about this false but persistent smear:

What's True

During a Feb. 28, 2020, campaign rally in South Carolina, President Donald Trump likened the Democrats' criticism of his administration's response to the new coronavirus outbreak to their efforts to impeach him, saying "this is their new hoax." During the speech he also seemed to downplay the severity of the outbreak, comparing it to the common flu.

What's False

Despite creating some confusion with his remarks, Trump did not call the coronavirus itself a hoax. [163]

In fact, the Donald J. Trump for President campaign actually filed a lawsuit [164] to halt the false smear being broadcast on television in a political campaign by a Democrat-leaning super PAC.

Fact-Checker.org – you know who they really are. No? Me neither. Nobody knows who they actually are, behind a clever name – has to admit:

"Trump did use the word 'hoax' but his full comments, and subsequent explanation, make clear he was talking about Democratic attacks on his administration's handling of the outbreak, not the virus itself." [165]

Similarly, FactCheck.org also exposed this distraction as a falsehood, in my words a smear. [166]

Correspondent Scott Pelley responded, "He said that the Democrats making so much of it is a Democratic hoax, not that the virus was a hoax."

Very recently, the Associated Press also (again) fact checked this myth as false on September 17, 2020: [167]

> THE FACTS: The accusation and the selective video editing are misleading. At the rally featured in the video, Trump actually said the phrases "the coronavirus" and "this is their new hoax" at separate points. Although his meaning is difficult to discern, the broader context of his words shows he was railing against Democrats for their denunciations of his administration's coronavirus response.
>
> "Now the Democrats are politicizing the coronavirus," he said. "You know that, right? Coronavirus. They're politicizing it." He meandered briefly to the subject of the messy Democratic primary in Iowa, then the Russia investigation before returning to the pandemic. "They tried the impeachment hoax. ... And this is their new hoax."
>
> ***
>
> But it is incorrect for Biden to suggest, as the video does, that Trump insisted the virus was a hoax before ultimately acknowledging to the author in April that it was deadly and serious.

As Bill O'Reilly pointed out recently, why would President Trump shut down travel from China on January 31, 2020, if he thought that the coronavirus threat was only a hoax? Trump was attacked for acting too soon. Why would the President take such strong early measures to control COVID-19 if he believed it to be a hoax? That makes no sense, even for Trump critics.

So we know for a fact that Trump was not saying that the coronavirus is a hoax, because 24 days before in his State of the Union address – which Nancy Pelosi then ripped up on national television – Trump explained to the nation that he was taking it very seriously.

So what did Donald Trump actually say?

During a February 28, 2020, campaign rally in Charleston, South Carolina, in an informal partisan political context, Trump told the crowd: [168]

> "We are stronger. We are better. But while we are building a great future the radical left Democrats in Washington are trying to burn it all down. [crowd boos] They have spent the last three years, and I can even go further than that three years since the election, but we go before the election, working to erase your ballots and overthrow our democracy. But with your help we have exposed the far-left's corruption and defeated their sinister schemes. Let's see what happens in the coming months. Let's watch. Let's just -- just watch. "

"Very dishonest people."

"Now the Democrats are politicizing the coronavirus. You know that. Coronavirus. They are politicizing it. We did one of the great jobs. You say how is Trump doing. Oh not good. Not good. They have no clue. They don't have any clue. They can't even count their votes in Iowa. They can't even count... No, they can't...."

"They can't count their votes."

"One of my people came up to me and said Mr. President, they tried to beat you on Russia, Russia, Russia. That didn't work out too well. They couldn't do it. They tried the impeachment hoax. That was on a perfect conversation. They tried anything. They tried it over and over. They've been doing it since you got in. It's all turning. They lost. Its' all turning. Think of it. Think of it."

"And this is their new hoax. But we did something that's been pretty amazing. We have 15 people in this massive country. And because of the fact that we went early. We went early. We could've had a lot more than that. We're doing great. Our country is doing so great. We are so unified. We are so unified."

* * *

"So a number that nobody heard of that I heard of recently and I was shocked to hear it. 35,000 people on average die each year from the flu. Did anyone know that? 35,000. that's a lot of people. It can go to 100,000. It can be 27,000. They say usually a minimum of 27,000 people. It can go up to a high of 100,000 people. And so far we have lost nobody. We have lost nobody to coronavirus in the United States. Nope."

"And it doesn't mean we won't. And we are totally prepared. It doesn't mean we won't."

"But think of it. You hear 35 and 40,000 people. And we've lost nobody. You wonder. The press is in hysteria mode."

* * *

"We are magnificently, we really, you take a look, we are magnificently organized with the best professionals in the world. We're prepared for the absolute worst. You have to be prepared for the worst. But hopefully it will amount to very little. "

"That's why I tell you when we have the flu at 35,000 people, and this one uh we have to take it very, very seriously. That's what we are doing. We are preparing for the worst."

"My administration has taken the most aggressive action in modern history to prevent the spread of this illness in the United States. We are ready. We are ready. Totally ready."

"On January 31, I ordered the suspension of foreign nationals who have recently been in China from entering the United States."

"An action which the Democrats loudly criticized and protested. And now everybody is complimenting me and saying thank you very much you were 100% correct. "

"Could've been a whole different story. I said, let's get this right. A virus starts in china, spread its way into various countries all around the world, does not spread widely at all in the United States because of the early actions that myself in my administration took against a lot of other wishes."

"And the democrats single talking point, and you see it, is that it's Donald Trump's fault, right? Now, just things happen. Things happen. Whoever thought of this. Two weeks ago who would've thought this would be going on, four weeks ago? But things happen in life and you have to be prepared and you have to be flexible and have to be able to go out and get it."

"My guys, we have the best professionals in the world, the best in the world and we are so ready. At the same time that I initiated the first federally mandated quarantine in over 50 years, we had to quarantine some people. They were not happy. They weren't happy about it. There are a lot of people not so happy but after two weeks they got happy. You know who got happy, the people around them got happy."

"I also created a white house virus task force. Is a big thing."

"I requested $2.5 billion to ensure we have the resources we need. The democrats said that's terrible. H'es doing the wrong thing. He needs 8.5 billion. I ask for $2.5 billion. I said, I'll take it. I'll take it. Never had that before. And I never had it. We want $2.5 billion. That's plenty. We demand you take $8.5 billion. He doesn't know what he's doing."

NO, TRUMP DID NOT FIRE THE PANDEMIC RESPONSE TEAM

A major and persistent lie is that President Trump fired the head of the nation's "pandemic response team" and disbanded the pandemic unit. As a result, the United States was not prepared to respond to .... well.... respond to the tiny trickle of rumors that China was actively hiding and suppressing as we have seen elsewhere and the official pronouncements by the World Health Organization that there was apparently no "human to human transmission" of the coronavirus, signaling in effect "nothing to see here, no big deal, never mind, nothing to worry about" as my translation.

First, the truth is that no one was fired. Some people *quit*, apparently because they were not happy that Trump won the 2016 election. It appears that they did not want to work for the Trump Administration and so they left the White House's National Security Council.

When John Bolton became National Security Advisor, Rear Admiral Tim Ziemer resigned from the NSC.

The extremely left-wing rag HuffPost explained: "The departure comes amid a reshuffling of the NSC under newly named national security adviser John Bolton, which includes a change in organizational structure that eliminates the office Ziemer led. Ziemer's staff has been placed under other NSC departments. [169] "And: "According to Robert Palladino, NSC spokesman, the reorganization will streamline the process, and he said Ziemer left "on the warmest of terms." *Id.*

Second, the unit within the National Security Council was re-organized by John Bolton, who was then Donald Trump's new National Security Advisor (after Gen. Michael Flynn was pushed out).

The unit was not disbanded. It is still there now. A re-organization of a government unit means that maybe the name gets changed. Maybe the structure is rearranged. Maybe it reports to a different superior.

But re-organized is not disbanded.

Tim Morrison debunked the lie in a column in *The Washington Post*. [170]

> ... Because I led the very directorate assigned that mission, the counterproliferation and biodefense office, for a year and then handed it off to another official who still holds the post, I know the charge is specious.

> * * *

> When I joined the National Security Council staff in 2018, I inherited a strong and skilled staff in the counterproliferation and biodefense directorate. This team of national experts together drafted the National Biodefense Strategy of 2018 and an accompanying national security presidential memorandum to implement it; an executive order to modernize influenza vaccines; and coordinated the United States' response to the Ebola epidemic in

Congo, which was ultimately defeated in 2020.

It is true that the Trump administration has seen fit to shrink the NSC staff.

But the bloat that occurred under the previous administration clearly needed a correction. Defense Secretary Robert Gates, congressional oversight committees and members of the Obama administration itself all agreed the NSC was too large and too operationally focused (a departure from its traditional role coordinating executive branch activity).

As The Post reported in 2015, from the Clinton administration to the Obama administration's second term, the NSC's staff "had quadrupled in size, to nearly 400 people." That is why Trump began streamlining the NSC staff in 2017.

One such move at the NSC [171]was to create the counterproliferation and biodefense directorate, which was the result of consolidating three directorates into one, given the obvious overlap between arms control and nonproliferation, weapons of mass destruction terrorism, and global health and biodefense.

It is this reorganization that critics have misconstrued or intentionally misrepresented. If anything, the combined directorate was stronger because related expertise could be commingled.

The reduction of force in the NSC has continued since I departed the White House. But it has left the biodefense staff unaffected — perhaps a recognition of the importance of that mission to the president, who, after all, in 2018 issued a presidential memorandum to finally create real accountability in the federal government's expansive biodefense system.

John Bolton – recently a Trump critic -- also responded:

John Bolton ✔
@AmbJohnBolton

Claims that streamlining NSC structures impaired our nation's bio defense are false. Global health remained a top NSC priority, and its expert team was critical to effectively handling the 2018-19 Africa Ebola crisis. The angry Left just can't stop attacking, even in a crisis.

11:05 AM · Mar 14, 2020 · Twitter for iPhone

1.7K Retweets   1.3K Quote Tweets   5.4K Likes

The original "Never Trump" *National Review* analyzed and reported: [172]

In January 2017, there were directorates for nonproliferation and arms control, for weapons of mass destruction and terrorism, and for global health security and biodefense. Bolton merged the three directorates into a "counterproliferation and biodefense" directorate.

According to administration officials I spoke with, this reorganization was designed in part to have better cooperation between those monitoring and preparing for intentional biological threats on one hand and for naturally occurring biological threats on the other. This directorate is now headed by Anthony Ruggiero.

In fact, the reorganization of a president's NSC is standard. Consider President Obama's NSC. He presided over the largest NSC in the nation's history; during the first part of his administration, some of his cabinet officials were frustrated by the NSC's overbearing micromanagement. Obama's national-security adviser, Susan Rice, sought to make the NSC more efficient. She even counts as one of her accomplishments her downsizing of what was an excessively large organization. Practically speaking, her reorganization meant eliminating or absorbing various directorates.

As noted in the quote from Tim Morrison's rebuttal, the Trump Administration took strong, aggressive action before 2020 to improve our nation's ability to respond to a public health threat. President Trump issued a *Presidential Memorandum on the Support for National Biodefense* on September 18, 2018. [173]

Also in September 2018, Trump's White House issued its *National Biodefense Strategy*, stating in its Foreword: [174]

> It is a vital interest of the United States to manage the risk of biological incidents. In today's interconnected world, biological incidents have the potential to cost thousands of American lives, cause significant anxiety, and greatly impact travel and trade. Biological threats—whether naturally occurring, accidental, or deliberate in origin—are among the most serious threats facing the United States and the international community. Outbreaks of disease can cause catastrophic harm to the United States. They can cause death, sicken, and disable on a massive scale, and they can also inflict psychological trauma and economic and social disruption. Natural or accidental outbreaks, as well as deliberate attacks, can originate in one country and spread to many others, with potentially far-reaching international consequences.

The President also issued an *"Executive Order on Modernizing Influenza Vaccines in the United*

States to Promote National Security and Public Health," on September 19, 2019, to improve the ability of U.S. health care companies to respond to public health threats such as influenza.[175]

Third, pandemic response is the job of the Centers for Disease Control and Prevention, the U.S. Department of Health and Human Services, the National Institutes for Health, the Department of Homeland Security, and the military's National Center for Medical Intelligence (NCMI) under the Defense Intelligence Agency (DIA).

The "pandemic response team" people are talking about was a unit in the bloated Obama White House National Security Council. The National Security Council deals with military and terrorist threats and foreign policy – not public health.

So the "pandemic response team" they are talking about was *not* a "pandemic response team." That is the job of the CDC, HHS, NIH, DHS, and NCMI – *not* the National Security Council.

There was no change in the actual U.S. Government agencies responsible for monitoring public health threats and responding to them at the CDC, HHS, NIH, DHS, and NCMI. Everything and everyone in the correct government agencies for detecting, investigating, and responding to a growing pandemic threat remained completely untouched and the same as always.

Fourth, the problem was that China blocked the CDC from investigating the early signs of a then-seemingly-small curiosity. The problem was not the lack of a "pandemic response team." The problem was China refusing to allow the CDC in to investigate.

Did President Trump Save Two Million Americans?

As *The New York Post* reported on February 3, 2020: [176]

> China has so far refused to allow the CDC into the country to help on the coronavirus, the Trump administration says.
>
> "We continue to offer assistance to the Chinese. We have offered to send over the CDC and other US medical and public health officials," White House national security adviser Robert O'Brien told CBS TV's "Face the Nation" on Sunday. "We have not heard back yet from the Chinese on the offers, but we are prepared to continue to cooperate with them."

As *The New York Times* explained in "C.D.C. and W.H.O. Offers to Help China Have Been Ignored for Weeks:" [177]

> Privately, Chinese doctors say they need outside expertise. But Beijing, without saying why, has shown no interest so far.
>
> For more than a month, the Centers for Disease Control and Prevention has been offering to send a team of experts to China to observe its coronavirus outbreak and help if it can.

Normally, teams from the agency's Epidemic Intelligence Service can be in the air within 24 hours.

But no invitation has come — and no one can publicly explain why.

The World Health Organization, which made a similar offer about two weeks ago, appears to be facing the same cold shoulder, though a spokeswoman said it is just "sorting out arrangements."

The New York Times reported further:

The United States has offered Dr. Tedros 13 specialists who are ready to go, Mr. Azar said.

The two fields in which China appears to need outside help, experts said, are molecular virology and epidemiology.

The first involves sequencing the virus's genome and manipulating it to refine diagnostic tests, treatments and vaccine candidates.

The second involves figuring out basic questions like who gets infected and who does not, how long the incubation period is, why some victims die, how many other people each victim infects and how commonly hospital outbreaks are occurring.

"This isn't rocket science, it's basic stuff — but it's been five weeks and we still don't know the answers," one expert said.

It would be very useful, for example, to have a blood test for antibodies. That would make it possible to see how many infected people had recovered, which would make it clearer as to how lethal the virus is — and how widespread.

A major epidemiological failure by China is that the Wuhan authorities appear to have closed and disinfected the seafood market that was the outbreak's early focus without swabbing individual animals and their cages and without drawing blood from everyone working there. That would have provided a wealth of information about which animal might have been the source of the coronavirus and which people had become infected but survived.

Fifth, actually, Barack Obama expanded the National Security Council in the White House to over 400 members. This bloat included some staff focused on the risk of the Ebola and Swine Flu epidemics.

But they were in the National Security Council. Not the CDC. Not NIH. Not the Department of Health and Human Services. The National Security Council.

The problem of a bloated, redundant, over-bearing National Security Council in the Obama White House was reported as early as 2015 in *The Washington Post:* [178]

> When Susan E. Rice took over as President Obama's national security adviser two years ago, she was struck by how the White House had grown. Since she had last served on the National Security Council, during the Clinton administration, its staff had nearly quadrupled in size, to about 400 people.
>
> Earlier this year Rice embarked on an effort to trim that number, hoping to make the policy-making process more agile. By mid-July, she said in an interview, the staff had been cut by 6 percent.
>
> But it may be too late to change impressions of an NSC bureaucracy whose size has come to symbolize an overbearing and paranoid White House that insists on controlling even the smallest policy details, often at the expense of timely and effective decisions.

* * *

> Many inside Cabinet departments and agencies complain that their expertise and experience is undervalued and that they are subjected to the whims of less

knowledgeable NSC staffers. With such a large structure that in some areas duplicates their own departments, senior officials see the NSC as usurping their responsibilities, leaving them feeling unappreciated and frustrated.

"If assistant secretaries, deputy assistants, don't have a sense of authorship and accountability, they tend to get beaten down," said a recently departed high-level administration official. "When large agencies — the Defense Department or State or others — don't feel as much a part of the takeoff, implementation tends to suffer. It's just human nature."

Others are less diplomatic. "Any little twerp from the NSC can call a meeting and set the agenda," a senior State Department official said.

* * *

"Time seems to be all this process produces. More time, more meetings, more discussions," the official said.

Others fume that the NSC has taken over things that could and should be handled elsewhere in the government. Former CIA director and defense secretary Leon Panetta, who left the administration in February 2013, has spoken of the "increasing centralization of power at the White House" and a "penchant for control" that in his case included submission of speeches and interview requests for White House approval.

That was way back in 2015 in the middle of the Obama Administration. When Trump became President, John Bolton moved to improve the NSC, and shift responsibility back to the subject matter expert agencies where the authority belongs, like the CDC and NIH.

When a government office is restructured, the old unit is just folded into a new structure. The old directorate of global health security and biodefense was given a new name. But the unit was still there. Then some Obama hold-overs also resigned.

In fact, the New York Times published leaked emails [179] trying – and failing – to make it look like the Trump Administration was slow to act. What the emails do show is that the pandemic response team – that critics say was disbanded– was actively debating news of the Wuhan virus very early in January. The unit is still there.

Note: People forget that during the 2016 presidential campaign, there was an effort to make sure no foreign policy professionals or experts would support or work for Donald Trump, to try to keep him from being elected or if elected to implement his "America First" anti-globalist policy agenda.

Therefore, observing that Obama hold-overs in the foreign policy agencies like the National Security Council resigned after Donald Trump became President should hardly surprise anyone. Obama staffers moved on and did not stay to work for Trump. So what? Why is that an issue? As *Fortune Magazine* then reported: [180]

"In an open letter to Donald Trump, more than 70 Republican foreign policy experts have banded together to agree on one thing: Trump cannot become president."

"The letter, posted on foreign policy site War on the Rocks, said that Trump would make the United States "less safe" if elected president. The experts listed their gripes with the frontrunner's foreign policy platform, including his aggressive advocacy for waging trade wars—" a recipe for economic disaster"—and his inconsistent vision for the United States' role in global affairs."

A copy of the letter can be found at: WOTR Staff, "Open Letter On Donald Trump From GOP National Security Leaders," War on the Rocks, March 2, 2016. [181]

So foreign policy experts resigned after Trump took office. They were not fired. That's politics.

IMPEACHMENT MANAGERS "HAVE BLOOD ON THEIR HANDS"

September 24, 2019 to February 5, 2020
Democrats' impeachment hoax shuts down federal government
December -- China concealing COVID-19 pandemic

Those who hate Trump (but really they hate me and you) impeached President Trump on December 19, 2019. [182] The impeachment inquiry formally started on September 24, 2019.

It was not until December 31, 2019, that China revealed the Wuhan virus. But it was Adam Schiff's job as Chairman of the House Intelligence Committee to watch for threats overseas, including any evidence that China was suppressing information. Instead, Adam Schiff had turned the Intelligence Committee into the impeachment committee.

The impeachment involved the nation's foreign policy and intelligence communities. The (false) accusation against President Trump was engineered as a failed *coup d'etat* by members of the intelligence agencies coordinating with Adam Schiff. Democrats ransacked through those agencies looking for witnesses, documents, emails, text messages, etc., casting everyone under suspicion, including in Embassies around the world.

The foreign policy and intelligence establishments became politicized, scandal war zones. They were compromised. As a result, they were hindered from doing their jobs, under threat and suspicion and being investigated for any witnesses who could testify against Trump.

The sweetheart deals with China in particular with Joe Biden and his son Hunter Biden were under the microscope. Therefore, the very agencies and officials who we needed to be reading between the lines in China's words, actions, and behavior were instead focused on Adam Schiff's de facto impeachment committee on Capitol Hill.

On January 15, 2020, the Democrat-controlled House ceremoniously signed and delivered the Articles of Impeachment to the Senate. Nancy Pelosi handed out commemorative pens (perhaps made in China).

That triggered a mandatory trial in the U.S. Senate. Senators were required by Senate rules to sit in their seats and listen. They were not allowed to speak. [183] So the Senate committees run by Republicans could barely meet or operate until February 5, 2020, when the Senate trial ended. The Chief Justice presided.

Most of official Washington was paralyzed by the impeachment farce from September 24, 2019, through February 5, 2020.

Trump's critics are trying to move the goal posts and claim that Trump was warned during January.

(He wasn't until late January.) But they ignore the fact that they were the ones trying to impeach him during December and January. They brought the federal government to a halt and distracted its leadership. People died. To use the same arguments brought against Trump, Democrat party impeachment managers killed 214,081 Americans.

As *Politico* explained about official Washington's response to the growing threat from COVID-19 from China:

> "On Jan. 24, at the urging of Sen. Lamar Alexander (R-Tenn.), administration officials held a briefing for the full Senate. But the classified session was sparsely attended, two Senate aides said, because it was put together at the last minute and was held on the same day as a deadline for senators to submit their impeachment questions. Only about 14 of them showed up." [184]

Note that Sen. Alexander is the Chairman of the U.S. Senate Committee on Health, Education, Labor & Pensions. Therefore, the disease epidemic falls within Sen. Alexander's jurisdiction in the U.S. Senate as Chairman of that Committee. By the way, how much have you heard from Senator Alexander during all of this crisis? How much have we heard from any Republican Senator besides Lindsey Graham and Thom Tillis?

Your author worked at the U.S. Department of Education when Sen. Alexander was Secretary of Education, during "America 2000." Senator Alexander's dignified inactivity today is no surprise. Lamar Alexander is not the sort of man to understand that it is his job to actually do something, other than just standing there and sounding calm and reassuring.

The Chair of the U.S. Senate Intelligence Committee is Republican Richard Burr (R-NC). For all we know from his complete invisibility, Burr could have died years ago, like the movie "Weekend at Bernie's." If the Republican answer on the Senate side to Adam Schiff on the House side were to disappear invited to travel on a visiting flying saucer, it is possible that no one would notice.[185]

So Republican Senators also did nothing to detect, investigate, or respond to the growing threat from Wuhan in Hubei Province, even in the U.S. Senate Intelligence Committee and the Committee on Health (Etc.). The point of being a Republican Senator is to be admired and looked-up to as being "dignified" in home-town parades. Their job is to very vigorously and impressively do nothing at all.

On the other side of Capitol Hill, the U.S. House of Representatives has been dominated by Trump-haters obsessed with over-turning the 2016 election and completing a "fundamental transformation of America."

No one was minding the store when the horses were leaving the barn. And now we are up a remote creek without a paddle.

TRUMP GAVE REASSURING HOPE
WILL TAKING STRONG ACTION

The Only Thing We Have to Fear is Fear Itself. *FDR*

"Facts don't care about your feelings."
-- Ben Shapiro

When is a national emergency not an emergency?

On January 31, 2020, President Donald Trump declared a national Public Health Emergency through Secretary of Health and Human Services Alex Azar. An ***EMERGENCY***. The President of the United States officially pronounced an *EMERGENCY*.

So what part of *AN EMERGENCY* do Trump's critics not understand?

They accuse Trump of not being hysterical enough. Trump didn't take the COVID-19 threat seriously enough (even though that hadn't actually happened yet beyond Hubei Province, China).

How much more seriously can a President take something than **"IT's AN EMERGENCY!!"** ?

On January 27, 2020, completely exposing and discrediting the outright lies of the President's critics, President Donald J. Trump announced to the nation and the world that the virus was a danger and that the Trump Administration was "strongly on watch" even though there were then only "very few cases reported in the USA." [186] Remember that Trump's Twitter account is followed by 86.1 million people in the United States and around the world, including journalists.

We are in very close communication with China concerning the virus. Very few cases reported in USA, but strongly on watch. We have offered China and President Xi any help that is necessary. Our experts are extraordinary!

9:56 AM · Jan 27, 2020 · Twitter for iPhone

21.4K Retweets   **1.5K** Quote Tweets   **115.6K** Likes

January 27. That was way back on January 27.

Therefore, it is a monstrous lie to suggest that Trump did not alert the American people to the dangers of the virus. It is a monstrous lie to argue that the President was not on top of the threat at the very earliest of stages.

On February 4, 2020, in the State of the Union Address before both houses of Congress assembled together. [187] Although all State of the Union addresses are a series of very short, bullet point topics covering a broad scope of different things all around the world, Trump told the entire nation on February 4, 2020, that his Administration was watching the growing threat from the China virus very closely and talking to China and would take strong action in response to the virus.

Trump's critics are saying that Trump failed to warn the American people.

Umm, an _**emergency**_? That didn't tip them off? The American people wouldn't figure out that something was going on when President Trump called it a Public Health Emergency?

Way back on January 31, 2020.

And Trump addressed the seriousness of the COVID-19 pandemic – if briefly (as is the norm for any topic in any State of the Union speech) – on February 4, 2020.

The constant refrain that Trump was slow to respond is like everything else coming out of our now thoroughly corrupt national politics: A total lie.

Donald Trump and the Trump Administration acted early and powerfully to respond to the spread of a new disease in Hubei Province, China.

But the President also fulfilled his proper role of trying to calm and reassure the public.

Trump talked to the public in calming tones.

Behind the scenes and in official actions, Trump was scrambling like a whirling dervish to respond to the new coronavirus that causes COVID-19.

Strong actions.

Calming words.

Sort of like "Speak softly and carry a big stick." – President Teddy Roosevelt.

Guess what? No, the President did not run around holding his head with his hands screaming in panic and hysteria, as if his "hair was on fire."

Guilty as charged. Trump did not weep like a baby and scream "We're all gonna die!"

Remember when President Franklin Delano Roosevelt shrieked "We're all going to die!" during the Great Depression? After Pearl Harbor? No, I don't remember that, either. Can you imagine man's man Teddy Roosevelt expressing pessimism about anything or biting his finger nails about some problem?

It is a national leader's job to give hope, to give people confidence. To help focus people on effective action, not getting distracted.

A nation, a business, an army battalion, any team is unlikely to succeed if they are self-absorbed with despair, pessimism, gripped with fear, and convinced of failure. Reassuring the nation is more than just feelings. Maintaining optimism and calm is essential to success. The nation needs to focus on the problem, not be emotionally distracted by uncertainty and fright.

If a nation's leader does not help us keep it together, the nation cannot fight the virus and deliver therapies and a vaccine. (For an illustration, see the TV series "The Last Ship," showing the collapse of society after a worldwide, lethal viral pandemic. Even after they have a vaccine in the show, they cannot deliver it because society has broken down into chaos.)

But his critics are selling the assumption that If Trump's words conveyed hope, that means he could not have been doing anything within the machinery of government. He must not have been doing anything if he was not openly panicking and predicting catastrophe.

Trump did what a national leader is supposed to do: Signal that

"We will get through this."

But that's what Trump's critics are blaming him for failing to do: Trump couldn't possibly truly care unless he is panicking and sobbing on the floor pounding the carpet with his fists or curled up in the fetal position in the corner.

Because that's what Leftists do. They are obsessed with feelings, not so much with logic.

Remember Apollo 13? Yes, the movie but it was the same in real life: After the shocking revelation -

> *"Houston, we are venting something out into space. I can see it outside Window 1 right now .... It's definitely a gas of some sort. ... It's gotta be the oxygen."*

Flight Director Gene Kranz takes firm control and quiets the explosion of voices, chaos, and emotion:

> "Quiet down. *Quiet down!* Let's stay cool people. .... Let's work the *problem*, people. Let's not make things worse by ... *guessing.*"

That's what conservatives and I think most well-grounded, normal Americans want:

A leader who stays cool under pressure.

But that's not what Leftists want. Leftists want someone to express their emotions, to scream at the sky with them, and help them feel the catharsis of screaming "This is the end! It's Mad Max at Thunderdome!" "The Walking Dead is here !"

So we have a clash of leadership styles. Trump is of the school that says a leader eliminates the fog of emotion and zeroes in on solutions:

Take things one step at a time. Take deep breaths. Count to ten. Clear your mind. Work the problem. Don't get distracted.

Critics truly want Star Trek's emotional Dr. McCoy not logical Mr. Spock. "Damn it, man, don't you care people are dying???" They are baffled that we don't see it their way.

Indulge me but I can't shake the example of the spaceship pilot in the science fiction TV series "Firefly" set some 500 years in the future.

"Wash" – the pilot – is skittish and whiny, and a weenie, wimpy, most of the time.

But in a crisis, he suddenly becomes cool as ice, calm as cold steel with an iron constitution, as he smoothly dodges all the space debris and safely lands the crippled spaceship. The contrast creates an image of taking control.

But the criticisms imply that Trump was not taking effective action. How could he? They are assuming:

- Only someone who is panicking appreciates the seriousness of the situation.

- Only someone who believes the problem is an extreme, end of the world, severely serious crisis is doing anything about it.

- They would have screamed at NASA Flight Director Gene Kranz: *"Don't you care ??"*

- Therefore, Trump could not have been doing anything to fight the spread of the virus,

- Because Trump was calm and
  giving reassuring hope to the
  American people.

Ironically, the airwaves are filled with TV
commercials as feel good messages from private
business and Public Service Announcements
offering the same positive message such as "We are
all in this together," complete with parents dancing
with their children at home, lovely, uplifting music,
and offering hope. Even as businesses having
nothing to do with the topic share hope and good
feelings, Trump is attacked for assuring the country
that we will overcome this national challenge, too,
as we have others.

They argue by strong implication that people are
dead because Trump "downplayed" the disease. If
only Trump had said the words "**This is serious,
folks, this is really, really bad**," then the virus
would have been watching the TV network news
and would have turned around and left our country
alone.

Critics actually push the idea, but without
explicitly saying it, that the disease would have
gone away if Trump just *cared* enough.

Note: They said the same things about Ronald
Reagan and AIDS. To this day, Left-wingers will
insist to you, right now if you prompt them, that
people died of AIDS because Reagan did not *talk*
about AIDS enough. Leftists have literally argued to
me that people died of AIDS because Reagan didn't
care about people with AIDS. AIDS spread because
Reagan did not stand up and *care* about AIDS.

And they are not saying that people were not
warned, because AIDS was being talked about all
the time back then. Everyone knew about it. Reagan

actually did care, of course, but their arguments are irrational. Reagan downplayed AIDS. Sound familiar? And that's what kills people. Not from a disease, but because the President doesn't care.

Trump is a doer. He rarely sleeps. Even if you want to call him arrogant, his pride makes him determined to overcome any challenge. Trump is stubborn. He does not let anything or anyone beat him. One thing you cannot say about Trump is that he is apathetic.

Yet, for example, CBS News broadcast and posted a video TV news report "Trump Downplays Coronavirus Threat In U.S. While Talking Up Administration's Response" on February 27, 2020. [188]

Notice how CBS News admits "while talking up administration's response" Words vs. Action. The news media knows that. They are merely lying.

To further this irrational attack on Trump, *The Washington Post* put together a video montage in "54 times Trump downplayed the coronavirus." [189]

This is illustrated by CNN's post "Trump repeatedly downplayed the virus as the US reopened." [190] CNN reports as the introduction to a video news report posted there: "President Donald Trump has repeatedly delivered positive remarks on the United States' coronavirus response despite more than 4 million cases and nearly 150,000 deaths."

That's sort of a leader's job, to "repeatedly deliver [] positive remarks." CNN's criticism is that as the leader of a nation, Trump was supposed to deliver pessimistic, fatalistic, defeatist remarks? Really?

The New York Times published an opinion piece titled "A Complete List of Trump's Attempts to Play Down Coronavirus: He could have taken action. He didn't.," on March 15, 2020. [191] As we have seen – just not true.

But this criticism flows from an entirely different mentality. To understand this requires experience with and an understanding of Leftists.

Leftists live in a world of their feelings.

"Never Trumper" establishment Republicans live in a world of abject terror that Leftists might criticize them. So the "Patty Hearst Republicans" with Stockholm Syndrome also slavishly believe whatever lie the Left spins. "Yes, Massa!" the GOP establishment echoes. "How high?" D.C. Republicans ask when Leftists scream "Jump!"

On February 24, 2020, Trump said that there were only 15 cases, that the virus was under control, and the virus should soon be gone. *That was true when Trump said it*, until a second wave of the virus arrived from Europe. Most cases were in quarantine after people returned home from overseas. They went into isolation or quarantine.

That was two days before the first confirmed case originating in the United States. By February 29, 2020, there were only three known cases of infection occurring within the country rather than people infected overseas then travelling back home to the U.S.A.

It is astonishing how many critics of Donald Trump seek to weaken support for him by saying "Donald Trump doesn't care about you."

Trump supporters do not care if Trump cares about them. Conservatives are not looking for someone to care about us. Conservatives have family, friends, church, and God. Liberals need substitutes for God and even family. Leftists need someone to care about them.

Ordinary Americans want a national leader to do a *job*. Getting things done is the job. *Therapy is not the job.* We want President Donald Trump to *do* things, not to make us *feel* things.

Even establishment Republicans from the D.C. Swamp want candidates whom they can point to, and look up to, put on a pedestal and *feel* good about. They want someone they can revere as better than the average person.

Normal Americans are disgusted with how establishment Republicans look at the world. We want politicians who *do* things – who get things done -- not who stand around being admired. Roll up your sleeve, get grease under your fingernails, do some darn work.

The establishment of the Republican Party is horrified by such ideas. They don't expect a politician to *do* anything. They want elected officials who just stand there and look good with perfect hair and are superior examples of the sophisticated upper crust, upper classes of high society. Leftists cannot influence voters whom they do not understand.

CONSULT YOUR DOCTOR FOR MEDICAL ADVICE AND INFORMATION

It should be obvious: But these days nothing is common sense. It is necessary to be clear what should not need to be explained. Those who are spreading the lies about the President of the United States will also do anything to stop their lies from being exposed. You know how people broadcasting the truth are being banned, black-listed and censored.

This is not a book about giving health or medical advice. Watch: Left-wing social media companies and news media will try to censor it anyway.

Anyone with medical concerns should consult their doctor. No one should be evaluating symptoms or risks from the coronavirus threat or deciding on any treatment concerning COVID-19 without taking a doctor's advice.

This book explores governmental and policy responses to the COVID-19 crisis. In order to evaluate how quickly and how well the Trump Administration responded to the growing pandemic at its (a) early rumor stage when China was hiding and suppressing news of the disease and even "disappearing" Chinese doctors to silence them, (b) the early outbreak in Wuhan, China, (c) the stage of first international spread, (d) the first incidences of cases contracted in the United States, (e) outbreaks in New York, New Jersey, and New Orleans after Mardis Gras, and (f) the nationwide epidemic that developed -- we examine *what were the options*.

There are many books and speakers analyzing the medical aspects of this pandemic and potential treatments.

However, our question here is what would a reasonable and prudent President do when faced with the information available and the choices available.

To analyze whether Trump did a good job or not, we have to confront the conflicting medical and public health information. In this book, the reason for pointing out inconsistent opinions about COVID-19 is not to tell you what you should do about your personal health. The discussion here is that a reasonable president would be faced with differences of opinion as to the health dangers and the possible actions.

A decision-maker would have to sort out public health experts who did not agree with each other, in whole or in part. Pointing to only one side of a discussion would not illuminate the decisions facing a president. The President's job was to choose what to do from diverse opinions.

Back in January 2020, and at every stage after that, there were plenty of reasons to wonder which expert to listen to. A President had to figure out what to do about massive disagreement among various voices.

One of the excuses for censoring positive news about this President's handling of the health crisis is that medical advice – even if documented to be true – does not match the pronouncements of the World Health Organization. So the Leftist media and social media platforms are censoring anything that disagrees with W.H.O.

Governmental responses to a public health crisis need to consider the available options. Magic is not one of the options for dealing with a pandemic. Prayer is, but much of the criticisms against Donald Trump require magical thinking.

So let's be clear: Health issues involving COVID-19 are not a "do it yourself" project. You don't get medical advice from Facebook, Twitter, your neighbor on the street, a book, random, people, etc. Go see your doctor. Or a walk-in first aid clinic (what my father refers to affectionately as a "doc in a box.")

I am not aware of any medication or treatment relating to COVID-19 that you can take without first seeing a doctor, individually, to evaluate you and your circumstances and getting a prescription or doctor's orders.

Your author's father before retiring was a long-time physician. I published an article in the American Thinker on May 23, 2020, titled "Coronavirus Basics Too Many People Never Learned," [192] after consulting with Daniel W. Nebert, M.D., among the "top 10 finalists" for the Nobel in Physiology / Medicine in 2017. My article reminded readers that:

> "But medications that are not over-the-counter require a doctor's prescription. A physician evaluates a patient and screens for risk factors, allergies to medications, or other 'contraindications.' In Trump's case, the White House Physician Sean Connolly – not Pelosi – would decide if Trump's weight argues against the medication or whether hydroxychloroquine makes sense in

decreasing the President's chance of coronavirus infection."

And also:

"Doctors informed by this growing body of research decide who should get a prescription and who shouldn't. There are reasons why a doctor's prescription is required. This is not just "make work" to make doctor's practice their handwriting. Some people are not the right candidates for a particular drug."

You should not be using any book as your guide for medical treatment, except perhaps for one bit of advice:

"You need to see a doctor."

Don't guess....

"You need to see a doctor."

THE DISEASE IS NOT THE VIRUS THE VIRUS IS NOT THE DISEASE

Let's also take a moment to fully understand the context of what we are talking about. Trust me. This will help.

It will help to understand clearly that the virus is called SARS-CoV-2 and the disease that – *sometimes* – results from the virus is called COVID-19.

Again, this is not a book about the medical side of the COVID-19 disease. There are other books focused on that and there should be dozens more written in my opinion. Because there are so many big topics in play that are all important, this book is merely focused on the political lies and distortions about the U.S. Government's response to the threat of the virus. But we do need to pay attention to terminology and details of what we are talking about.

Do you care? Well, I didn't care for a long time. People kept beating me up when I would talk about the COVID-19 virus. I thought to myself "Yeah, yeah, whatever." I would continue to talk about the COVID-19 virus, which is wrong. I didn't think it mattered.

But slowly I started to understand what they were saying. Yes, you should carefully understand the difference. Yes, it does matter. It is extremely important.

The reason is because tens of millions of people have been exposed to the SARS-CoV-2 virus. But only a small percentage of them came down with the disease.

You can be exposed to a virus. You can test positive for having the virus in your system. *And yet you might not get the disease.*

No one can get sick from the disease COVID-19 without being exposed to the SARS-CoV-2 virus.

But not everyone exposed to a virus contracts a disease resulting from it. The vast majority of people who are exposed to or even infected with the SARS-CoV-2 virus will never get the COVID-19 disease.

Medical researchers are diligently trying to learn more about all of these things. Researchers are still trying to pin down fully why not everyone gets AIDS if they are exposed to the Human Immunodeficiency Virus (HIV).

Eventually, all of the 331 million people who live in the United States are likely to be exposed to SARS-CoV-2. There is nothing to stop that, other than God after national repentance from sin and national, corporate prayer. It might take a year. It might take 10 years. 100 years. But there is little or nothing we can do to prevent every human being in the United States from being exposed to the virus. What we can do is deal with the consequences, by helping the body bat the virus back out with a vaccine and treating any symptoms or effects.

Contrary to the very strong and very wrong assumptions among the public, most people exposed to the virus SARS-CoV-2 will never get sick.

Some people will be exposed to the virus, but it will not affect the person in sufficient quantity to make an impact. The body will shrug it off before the virus really gets a foothold.

With other people, they will truly get infected with the virus, but it may not produce a disease response. They may never get COVID-19 even though they have the virus. That sometimes happens even with HIV and AIDS.

That does not mean that they will get sick but have no noticeable symptoms. That happens a lot. A gigantic number of people will have symptoms from actually contracting the disease which are so mild that they don't notice them or pay attention. They may just feel run down as if they didn't get enough sleep or had a stressful week or are coughing, they think, due to pollen. So many people may actually be sick with COVID-19 and actually have real symptoms, but the symptoms are not so noticeable during the ups and downs of life that they notice and think about maybe having COVID-19.

A massive number of people who actually get sick with COVID-19 will have no symptoms at all. It is not just that the symptoms aren't noticed, but the symptoms are not there.

There are a very small number of people who contract COVID-19 who have a catastrophic reaction, sometimes even as a delayed response. COVID-19 can produce a disastrous pneumonia such that the victim loses the ability to breathe.

Note the severe harm to the lining of the lungs is like a pneumonia in damaging the ability of the lungs to process oxygen in and carbon dioxide out but might be thought of a little bit differently from pneumonia. Meanwhile, pneumonia even bacterial pneumonia can often be a byproduct of various kinds of diseases, especially among the elderly. So standard pneumonia can become a complication that severely hinders a patient. It can be a symptom or parallels illness.

It is currently believed that the main catastrophic death spiral involves a "cytokine storm"[193] in which the cells massively over-react causing catastrophic harm. [194] Cells can signal for help from the immune system. When a cell signals for help, it is under attack, the immune system sends T-cells, antibodies, etc.

But for some reason in various disease contexts, sometimes the immune response goes crazy. The cells create a cascading excessive response, causing enormous numbers of healthy cells – like the lining of the lungs – to call for an excessive amount of help, and the excessive immune response ends up actually killing healthy cells – in vast quantities.

In the lungs this can create a death spiral of rapid deterioration. The lining of the lungs can become so damaged that it loses the ability to intake oxygen into the body or expel carbon dioxide. This is life-threatening. This is the reason for ventilators, or as some prefer to recommend, high-oxygen chambers. The damage to the lungs can lead to rapid and severe decline and swift death.

In fact, such a downward spiral can occur very suddenly after a patient has seemed to recover. Some patients seem to tolerate COVID-19 as a modest disease, get better, and then they decline again and are dead within days. This is certainly frightening.

Remember: The disease epidemic named SARS was caused by SARS-CoV-1. This virus is SARS-CoV-2. SARS means "Severe Acute Respiratory Syndrome." COVID-19 is a SARS disease. The coronavirus that caused SARS is of the same type as the coronavirus that causes COVID-19. It is primarily a *respiratory* illness.

This is where some of the controversy comes in. Many dissenters on the science and the medicine of COVID-19 – which is *not* the subject of this book mostly because there are many, many other voices on those complex topics – are trying to address why a person exposed to SARS-CoV-2 may or may not get the disease and may or may not enter a catastrophic death spiral.

Many say that public health officials and the medical community should focus on the very few patients who experience a disastrous death spiral and not on the vast majority of people who quickly and easily recover from a mild form of COVID-19.

There is also a lot of discussion of factors that may strengthen the body in its reaction to the virus. So a strong immune system at full functioning because of the full recommended daily dose of Vitamins C and D, as well as Zinc and Magnesium, is important.

No, vitamins do not "cure" COVID-19. Don't be ridiculous.

But vitamins and dietary minerals are critical to the fully-effective functioning of the body's immune responses. They help the body's immune system to operate at full efficiency and potency. General overall health is important. Exercise can keep the body at good working strength. No, exercise is not a cure. But the argument of some is that these things help the body function at its best.

The controversy is that a weak, sickly person is at greater risk because their body will not be as effective in beating back the virus when they are first exposed. A strong, healthy body has a better chance of defeating the virus or "clearing" the virus as doctors are expressing it than a person whose immune system is degraded by poor diet, obesity, fatigue, and/or other illnesses at work in their body at the same time. That's in part because this is a numbers game.

When a person is first exposed to a virus, the numbers of specimens will be relatively tiny. But the virus then goes to work multiplying itself by hijacking the machinery of the body's cells. The virus invades a cell and takes over and makes the cell manufacture more copies of itself. Therefore, the number of virus specimens rapidly multiplies, geometrically as they say.

So at every stage, especially very early, the more the body can kill off virus specimens successfully, the total number of virus specimens at work in their body may be drastically reduced. This may be one reason related to why some people shrug off COVID-19 easily while others are whacked hard by the disease and some die. If the body can nip the infection in the bud before it rages out of control, the infection can be kept to a minimum.

So, no, nobody is saying that all these things are a "cure." That would be nonsense. The issue is that anything that can tip the odds in the body's favor while fighting off the infection is better than a person being in a weakened state. You know. Get plenty of rest. Drink lots of fluids (perhaps to wash out toxins among other things). Orange juice (Vitamin C). Watch for fever and take immediate action if a fever gets too high. *The same things you have been hearing all of your life.*

No, these will not "cure" COVID-19. Don't be silly. But the controversies that are swirling are about strengthening the body and helping the body help itself.

The explanation from professionals is that when exposed to a virus, any virus, the body is in a war.

Each and every specimen of the virus that the body can kill or expel is one step closer to winning the battle. It's a numbers game... with a 'geometric' acceleration component.

The body fights back killing the viral infection one by one until the virus is completely killed off or "cleared." Therefore, there are many things that help a patient's body fight back and kill off the virus, maybe before it even gets a foothold, that are not a "cure" but are helpful in winning the war.

Finally, many are tripping over words like a "cure." We don't typically "cure" a virus. We don't "cure" the flu. We treat the symptoms. We help the body win the battle. The body kills off the virus. We give the body every advantage in doing that. My father always says that physicians help the body heal itself. So we have debates about whether something is a "cure" or not. That is a confusion of terminology.

We should not let people confuse the conversation by tripping over the word "cure" or playing games between medications or treatments that treat the symptoms or provide therapy.

Treating symptoms is not technically a "cure." But anything that gives the body an advantage in "clearing" the virus by killing the virus specimens one by one contributes toward winning the war for the body to heal itself.

Now, unfortunately, the reality is that the virus is going to eventually reach the entire human race. Most people won't get sick. Most of those who get sick will have symptoms so mild they may not even notice. But over the coming years, everyone will be exposed to the SARS-CoV-2 virus.

Remember: The US Government recommended *"30 Days to Slow the Spread."* Not to *stop* the spread – because that is not possible. All of these measures were to *slow*—not stop—the virus spreading.

Remember: Everything we were and are doing was to "flatten the curve" – to stretch it out. That makes the spread *longer* in time.

Not even the most fervent advocates of government restrictions ever claimed that shutting down the economy, wearing masks, quarantines, lock-downs, (anti) social distancing would ever stop a single person from becoming infected with the SARS-CoV-2 coronavirus or sick.

The announced strategy was to just *slow down* this virus that was spreading at frightening speed – that is, at a very, very *unusual* rate for a virus. One of the characteristics of this virus is the astonishing ease and velocity with which it tears through a human population so rapidly.

But the strategy was to protect hospitals and medical resources from becoming over-whelmed. That is, the disease might be reasonably managed within the capacity of our hospitals and medical facilities and staffing. But if the sheer quantity of COVID-19 cases were to swamp the hospitals and equipment and resources, then the pandemic would become far more dangerous and deadly merely because the medical system could not handle the sheer numbers.

So the strategy was to "slow the spread" to keep the medical system from being strained beyond its capacity.

It was never claimed that (anti) social distancing and masks and lock downs would save even one person from getting the virus eventually. The plan was to manage the quantity of cases at any given time hitting the hospitals.

These measures would give us time to increase hospital beds and intensive care unit beds to meet the demand, build more ventilators, ramp up production of personal protective equipment (PPE), restock medicines and other medical supplies.

Delaying – not stopping – the spread would buy us time to try to rush a vaccine through invention, development, testing and production.

But even if wearing masks can slow down the spread of the virus, eventually the entire human population of the entire planet Earth will be exposed to the SARS-CoV-2 virus. We are blessed that the virus is so weak and almost no one gets seriously ill from it, because it will be impossible to stop it from reaching the entire human race.

Studies show that the virus is incredibly aerodynamic compared to its light weight. It has been observed to float in the air for as long as six (6) hours. Some studies suggest longer than six hours.

And then the virus can be kicked back up into the air. The virus is so light compared to its aerodynamic drag (remember the coronavirus name comes from its shape like a crown, with many rods poking out), that it can be sent back up into the air again. If the virus settles on the floor of a grocery store or office, the next person to walk through the dust along the floor can cause the virus to float back up into the air again. So it can become airborne again and again.

Studies indicate that the virus can stay potent on some kinds of objects and surfaces for as long as three (3) days. Some studies suggest as long as seventeen (17) days.

So, even if we can slow down the velocity at which the virus rips through society, no one is going to be spared from eventual exposure. It might take 1 year, 5 years, or 20 years, but the virus will reach every human alive.

Even if there is a vaccine, remember: A vaccine is just a deactivated form of the virus. The body reacts to the vaccine the same as it does to the actual virus. An impotent version of the virus allows the body to start creating anti-bodies and T-cells to kill off the virus. So, then, when the actual virus reaches that person, the body is ready and has a head start. The body's immune system can "get the jump on" the actual virus to use the language of 1940s cop and gangster movies.

But even with a vaccine, people will eventually be exposed to the actual, live virus. The vaccine will just empower that person's body to snuff it out as soon as the actual, live virus reaches them.

But, yes, the production of new copies of the virus comes from infected people. So those who have the vaccine will not generate many if any new copies of the virus, because the body will not have any substantial infection.

Vaccinated people will have a drastically reduced quantity in the production of the virus being created / replicated inside their bodies. So the quantity of the virus in society will be greatly reduced. Those protected by the vaccine will generate very few copies of the virus before the immune system bolstered by the advance warning of the vaccine "clears" the virus from the body as physicians say. A vaccinated person will not generate many copies of the virus. So widespread vaccination will greatly slow the spread of the virus throughout the human population but will not necessarily stop the spread entirely.

Remember: A virus works by invading and hijacking cells of the body, forcing the invaded cell to make copies of the virus. Cells are set up to create enzymes and DNA and RNA for normal functioning, and these mechanisms are forced to make copies of the virus instead.

So is it Trump's fault that a virus as a natural disaster does what viruses do? *"Viruses gonna virus,"* as Dr. Rodney Rohde from Texas State University explained. Dr. Rohde said: 'Once it kind of burns through the population, which is what viruses do, it will meet a collective human immune response." [195]

NATIONAL MANDATE TO WEAR UNIVERSALLY-REQUIRED MASKS?

U.S. Surgeon General ✓
@Surgeon_General

Seriously people- STOP BUYING MASKS!

They are NOT effective in preventing general public from catching #Coronavirus, but if healthcare providers can't get them to care for sick patients, it puts them and our communities at risk!
bit.ly/37Ay6Cm

7:08 AM · Feb 29, 2020 · Twitter for iPhone

62K Retweets and comments   **77.7K** Likes

On May 29, ABC News reported "CDC and WHO offer conflicting advice on masks. An expert tells us why. The two organizations have different takes on when to wear one." [196]   The article reports ""If you are healthy, you only need to wear a mask if you are taking care of a person with COVID-19," the WHO guidelines read."

Infectious disease expert Dr. Anthony Fauci told 60 Minutes on March 8, 2020: [197]

> "Right now people should not be wearing... there is no reason to be walking around with a mask. When you are in the middle of an outbreak wearing a mask might make people feel *[emphasized by Dr. Fauci's air quotes]* a little bit better and it might even block a droplet. But it is not providing the perfect protection that

> people think it is. And often there are unintended consequences. People keep fiddling with the mask, and they keep touching their face."

> "But when you think masks you should think of health care providers needing them and people who are ill."

The purpose of this chapter and this book is to analyze and dissect the attacks on the President of the United States.

This is not a discussion about whether or not people should wear "face coverings" from bandannas, to cloth tubes to flimsy masks to serious N95 or KN95 surgical masks to respirators.

The accusations are that President Trump should have ordered that everyone wear some form of "face coverings" nationwide, whether it makes sense in a local situation or not.

Former Vice President Joe Biden who is running for President against Donald Trump has made stinging accusations and offered proposals for how he would handle the COVID-19 pandemic.

Biden has very good proposals: They are Donald Trump's plans that Biden is plagiarizing. Biden promises if elected to do exactly what Donald Trump already did. His pitch to voters is to do what has already been done, early in the health crisis.

Biden's only real difference in his plans – is pledging to order nation-wide, universal, mandatory wearing of masks regardless of local situations for three months. Why three months? I would not expect an explanation.

So the issue is: Did Trump fail the American people by not ordering – ordering – the *mandatory* wearing of masks *before* any Democrat official admitted that there was anything to worry about.

So that is the question we are exploring: How can President Trump be blamed for not ordering a nationwide mask mandate when the experts keep changing their positions and arguments?

The case is certainly muddled and mixed. Is there a clear, compelling case that would compel a competent president to order everyone to wear masks? Confusion generated by Dr. Anthony Fauci, the Surgeon General of the United States, and other public health officials defeats any argument that President Donald Trump was irresponsible in not ordering the wearing of masks.

How can a political leader be faulted when medical experts keep flip-flopping themselves?

Now they are trying to back-pedal and argue that that was only during a time of limited supply. No, they were explicitly clear. Regardless of the available supply, the experts were against widespread mask wearing and then they were for it. Which is it? No, it was not about supply limitations. That is not what they said.

Remember? Experts said that the general public, not medically trained, tend to scratch their face under a mask, especially when masks are over-used instead of being replaced. (The inside of the mask tends to fray as it gets days old so the mask becomes increasingly itchy, as you might notice.) People then touch surfaces with their hands after scratching underneath the mask. So the mask can actually concentrate the virus in the fabric of the mask, from which it is then transferred in concentrated form by one's hand touching objects or even people.

Critics also say that that was then, this is now. What changed? Nothing.

On February 27, 2020, the Centers for Disease Control and Prevention advised against widespread wearing of masks by the general public. [198]

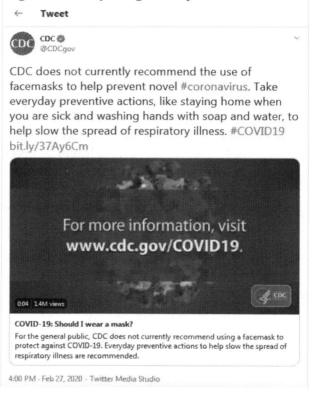

The CDC's information page says "Your cloth face covering *may* protect them. Their cloth face covering *may* protect you." *(emphases added)* [199] Notice "may."

Having no real argument as to why President Trump – or any president – can control a disease, Trump's critics fall back on arguing that Trump should have ordered a nationwide mask mandate.

As many times as it takes: This is not a discussion of whether to wear masks or not. The question is whether it is so *obviously* the one and only correct answer that Trump is at fault or failed by not ordering universal, mandatory mask wearing.

Your author lives in Virginia, where the State Government mandates the wearing of some face covering (vague) in order to go anywhere in public, to enter a store or restaurant (most of which are now take-out only). So I obey the law. I wear a mask. (I sometimes wear my Trump 2020 mask.)

I am certain that in early March – before testing was available without severe symptoms – I had COVID-19. It was just like a strong flu except that it left me exceedingly tired and groggy most of the day and night, for about 8 weeks, so that I could not think, and I fell behind on many responsibilities, getting late on my work. I took anti-biotics at the first hint of a slight congestion in my lungs that I felt reminded me of when I had light pneumonia a couple decades ago.

So I know I am not at risk of catching COVID-19 now. I am not contagious four months later. So I do not need to wear a mask. But the law requires me to, so I wear the darn mask.

However, it is a completely different question whether anyone can fault Trump for not ordering a nationwide mask mandate. Evaluating whether Trump did a good job is a totally different issue. This is a chapter here about whether it is right to *blame* any president for not ordering the universal, mandatory wearing of masks.

As many have commented: **"If your mask works, why do you care if I wear one?"**

Second, the President does not have any authority to order anyone to wear anything. See

Tinker v. Des Moines Independent Community School District, 393 U.S. 503, 89 S.Ct. 733, 21 L.Ed.2d 731 (1969).

This is explained in an article by attorneys John Yoo and Emanuel S. Heller. John Yoo is the Emanuel S. Heller Professor of Law at the UC Berkeley School of Law. Emanuel S. Heller Professor of Law at the University of California at Berkeley, a visiting scholar at the American Enterprise Institute, and a visiting fellow at the Hoover Institution, Stanford University. He is the author of Defender-in-Chief: Donald Trump's Fight for Presidential Power, to be published on July 28, and by James Phillips is an assistant professor of law at Chapman University's Fowler School of Law.

"There is nothing, however, that authorizes a President Trump now, or a President Biden tomorrow, to mandate face coverings nationwide via executive power. Congress has not enacted any such law for the president to enforce. Masks do not fall under the president's power as commander-in-chief, nor do they plausibly come within any of his other executive authorities, such as granting pardons or nominating officers."

"So the president must rely on Congress, which makes Speaker Pelosi's demands all the more rich given that the House has yet to mandate masks. She could try and claim some power under the Commerce Clause, which empowers

159

> Congress to "regulate Commerce . . . among the several States." The Founders wanted to prohibit the destructive state protectionism the states that had beset the nation during the early years of independence. Under the original meaning of the Commerce Clause, Congress might be able to require people crossing state lines, or within the streams of interstate commerce, to wear masks. It could even buy all Americans masks. But it cannot compel the large percentage of Americans who are not traveling to wear them." [200]

Trump does not have the power to issue a nationwide order that everyone wear a mask. Remember: When ObamaCare required that everyone must buy health insurance, Chief Justice of the U.S. Supreme Court John Roberts saved ObamaCare by redefining the mandate as a "tax." [201] It was so blatantly unconstitutional that the only way to save ObamaCare from itself was to pretend that the mandate to buy health insurance was not an order to buy health insurance at all but only a tax.

Now, Federal law is different from State law. Our U.S. Constitution grants power to the Federal government in only limited areas, but supreme in those areas over State laws. So State governments have much broader authority under the general "police power" than the U.S. Government. Where the U.S. Government legislates, its laws are supreme and pre-empt over State law. But there are things that the States can legislate that are broader than the scope of authority of the Federal government. So State governments might be able to require mask wearing where the Federal government cannot.

Third, quarantine laws, State and Federal, apply to the sick – not to the healthy. The power provided in public health laws aimed at contagious diseases are written to govern those who are actually sick or who have been exposed to an infectious or contagious disease.

Michigan's Supreme Court ruled on October 2, 2020, that heavy-handed, controversial Democrat Governor Whitmer's COVID-19 lockdown orders including mandates for masks and social distancing, violated the Michigan state constitution: [202]

> *Lansing* — In a landmark ruling with far-reaching implications, the Michigan Supreme Court decided Friday that Gov. Gretchen Whitmer violated her constitutional authority by continuing to issue orders to combat COVID-19 without the approval of state lawmakers.
>
> The state's high court ruled 4-3 that a state law allowing the governor to declare emergencies and keep them in place without legislative input — the 1945 Emergency Powers of the Governor Act — is unconstitutional.

A Federal district court struck down Pennsylvania's coronavirus orders as unconstitutional. [203]

A federal judge ruled on Monday that Pennsylvania Gov. Tom Wolf's (D) coronavirus orders, which shut down the state, closed businesses and limited gatherings, were unconstitutional.

U.S. District Judge William Stickman IV, a Trump appointee, said in his opinion that COVID-19 orders from Wolf and Pennsylvania Secretary of Health Rachel Levine violated and continue to violate the First Amendment right to freedom of assembly and the due process and equal protection clauses of the 14th Amendment.

The efforts to stop the spread of the coronavirus "were undertaken with the good intention of addressing a public health emergency," Stickman wrote.

"But even in an emergency, the authority of government is not unfettered," he added.

"There is no question that this Country has faced, and will face, emergencies of every sort," he wrote. "But the solution to a national crisis can never be permitted to supersede the commitment to individual liberty that stands as the foundation of the American experiment."

In Virginia, enforcement of quarantine laws requires that a person who is actually infected has already been warned that they are contagious. Only if such an actually infected person, having been warned, refuses to be quarantined, does Virginia State law give the Virginia government power to take any action. (During the hysteria, some judges blew past stop signs, stripped the gears, and upheld clearly invalid actions by Virginia's Governor.)

The requirement under the U.S. Constitution for due process in the law is violated if healthy people are quarantined or restricted with no indication that they are sick or actually exposed to an infection. No one can suffer deprivation of their liberty without some individualized proof that they may be dangerous to others by carrying a contagious disease. Due process cannot be satisfied by a blanket approach. There must be evidence specific to a particular person to suspend their liberties.

So can Donald Trump be blamed for not doing what would be unconstitutional, what he has no power to do? Consider South Dakota Governor Kristi Noem and her powerful speech to the Republican National Convention. Gov. Noem explained who she refused to order lockdowns like the rest of the nation during the coronavirus pandemic. She said that she listened both to health officials and to individuals who informed her about the bounds of her gubernatorial authorities.[204]

> "So I never issued a shelter-in-place, I never closed a business. I didn't even define an essential business ... because I don't have the authority to do that."

Did President Trump Save Two Million Americans?

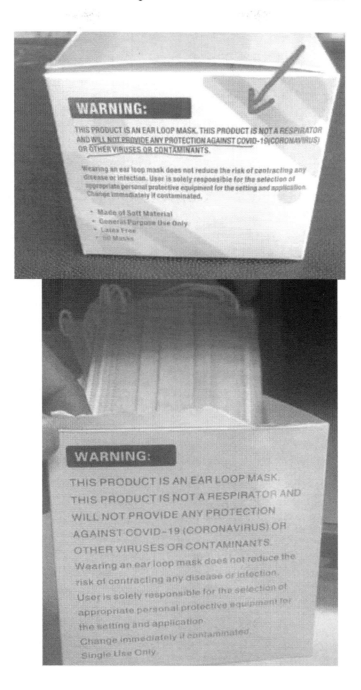

Fourth, do I need to say it again to avoid being banned and censored by Facebook or Amazon? We are not going to try to settle the medical debate over whether or not an entire society should wear masks as an effort never tried before in the history of humanity *(what is this science you speak of*???*)* as untested theory for controlling a contagious disease. We are going to focus on the wisdom or lack thereof of how the Trump Administration handled this challenge.

As Dr. Jim Meehan, MD explains: *[simple cloth]* "Medical masks are single use devices designed to be worn for a relatively short period of time. Once the mask becomes saturated with moisture from breath, which, if properly fit, takes about an hour, they should be replaced. The more moisture-saturated the mask becomes, the more it blocks oxygen, increases re-breathing of carbon dioxide, re-breathing of viral particles, and becomes a breeding ground for other pathogens." [205]

That is, in the medical field, the blue cloth masks everyone is using are *thrown away* and replaced with a new, clean mask about every hour or two. Doctors don't wear the same mask for days or weeks on end.

It is important to recognize that there is little scientific evidence on wearing masks throughout an entire society as a method of controlling disease. This has never been done before.

Remember that Dr. Anthony Fauci – who is *not* the head of the Centers for Disease Control nor even the head of the National Institutes for Health – picks and chooses when he supports ideas with no hard-core scientific proof and when he rejects out of hand solid studies that prove things Dr. Fauci does not like. Despite cries of following the science, the standards of science keep changing all the time depending on the preferences.

So in 1918, there is some anecdotal evidence that in some areas of the United States some people wore some form of face covering – certainly not as well-made or designed as today – and that perhaps, maybe it helped.

Yet the critics are quick to trash any documented proof of measures like hydroxychloroquine as only "anecdotal" or not up to gold-plated standards of randomized, double-blind studies in large numbers of randomly selected study patients over years. (This is actually unethical. Unlike like for drugs like weight loss or diabetes or baldness, a randomized study of patients who are actually sick with COVID-19 means that patients will likely die if they receive useless placebos rather than potentially life-saving medication or therapies.)

So by their own standards requiring random double-blind studies of randomly selected patients under the highest standards for study protocols, they would never tolerate stories from 1918 of undocumented stories that are basically hearsay.

As the New York Times reported on January 23, 2020, before the partisan political hit jobs against Trump started: [206]

> The risk of becoming infected with the coronavirus in the United States — where there is only one confirmed case — is "way too low to start wearing a face mask," said Dr. Peter Rabinowitz, who is co-director of the University of Washington MetaCenter

for Pandemic Preparedness and Global Health Security

* * *

The question is: do they work?

Many infectious disease specialists say the cheap disposable masks, which cover the nose and mouth, may help prevent the spread of infections if they are worn properly and used consistently.

But there isn't much high-quality scientific evidence on their effectiveness outside health care settings, experts say. Most of the best studies, which are randomized controlled trials, focused on how well surgical masks protect health care workers in hospitals from picking up infections from sick patients, and found that consistent use of them helped.

* * *

Because surgical masks aren't fitted or sealed, they leave gaps around the mouth, "so you're not filtering all of the air that comes in," she said.

Did President Trump Save Two Million Americans?

The Occupational Health and Safety Administration (OSHA) still today explains on its website, that *(emphases added)*: [207]

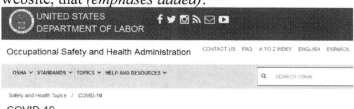

COVID-19 Frequently Asked Questions

This page includes frequently asked questions (FAQs) and answers related to the coronavirus disease 2019 (COVID-19) pandemic.

Cloth Face Coverings

What are the key differences between cloth face coverings, surgical masks, and respirators?

Cloth face coverings:

- May be commercially produced or improvised (i.e., homemade) garments, scarves, bandanas, or items made from t-shirts or other fabrics.
- Are worn in public over the nose and mouth to contain the wearer's potentially infectious respiratory droplets produced when an infected person coughs, sneezes, or talks and to limit the spread of SARS-CoV-2, the virus that causes Coronavirus Disease 2019 (COVID-19), to others.
- Are not considered personal protective equipment (PPE).
- Will not protect the wearer against airborne transmissible infectious agents due to loose fit and lack of seal or inadequate filtration.
- Are not appropriate substitutes for PPE such as respirators (e.g., N95 respirators) or medical face masks (e.g., surgical masks) in workplaces where respirators or face masks are recommended or required to protect the wearer.
- May be used by almost any worker, although those who have trouble breathing or are otherwise unable to put on or remove a mask without assistance should not wear one.
- May be disposable or reusable after proper washing.

Surgical masks:

- Are typically cleared by the U.S. Food and Drug Administration as medical devices (though not all devices that look like surgical masks are actually medical-grade, cleared devices).
- Are used to protect workers against splashes and sprays (i.e., droplets) containing potentially infectious materials. In this capacity, surgical masks are considered PPE. Under OSHA's PPE standard (29 CFR 1910.132), employers must provide any necessary PPE at no-cost to workers [1]
- May also be worn to contain the wearer's respiratory droplets (e.g., healthcare workers, such as surgeons, wear them to avoid contaminating surgical sites, and dentists and dental hygienists wear them to protect patients).
- Should be placed on sick individuals to prevent the transmission of respiratory infections that spread by large droplets.
- Will not protect the wearer against airborne transmissible infectious agents due to loose fit and lack of seal or inadequate filtration.
- May be used by almost anyone.
- Should be properly disposed of after use.

Cloth face coverings:

- May be commercially produced or improvised (i.e., homemade) garments, scarves, bandanas, or items made from t-shirts or other fabrics.
- Are worn in public over the nose and mouth to contain the wearer's potentially infectious respiratory droplets produced when an infected person coughs, sneezes, or talks and to limit the spread of SARS-CoV-2, the virus that causes Coronavirus Disease 2019 (COVID-19), to others.
- Are not considered personal protective equipment (PPE).
- **Will not protect the wearer against airborne transmissible infectious agents due to loose fit and lack of seal or inadequate filtration.**

Surgical masks:

- Are typically cleared by the U.S. Food and Drug Administration as medical devices (though not all devices that look like surgical masks are actually medical-grade, cleared devices).
- Are used to protect workers against splashes and sprays (i.e., droplets) containing potentially infectious materials. In this capacity, surgical masks are considered PPE. Under OSHA's PPE standard (29 CFR 1910.132), employers must provide any necessary PPE at no-cost to workers.[1]

- May also be worn to contain the wearer's respiratory droplets (e.g., healthcare workers, such as surgeons, wear them to avoid contaminating surgical sites, and dentists and dental hygienists wear them to protect patients).
- Should be placed on sick individuals to prevent the transmission of respiratory infections that spread by large droplets.
- **Will not protect the wearer against airborne transmissible infectious agents due to loose fit and lack of seal or inadequate filtration.**

Similarly, as explained by a chemist who has worked in the filtration industry, who helped develop masks used in medical and industrial settings and holds patents on several filters: [208]

> Surgical masks were not designed as filters and were not intended to be used as filters. Surgical masks were designed to be used by surgeons standing face down over an operating table holding a patient with an open wound. The surgeon wearing the mask would be able to talk to others in the room without discharging spittle droplets into the patient's wound. Spittle droplets are large and can cause infection.
>
> I witnessed a test of surgical masks. Small plaster particles were generated in a room. They were visible as a white dust in the air. A man was

properly fitted with a surgical mask and spent a short time in the room. When he came out, the mask was removed. A camera was focused on the man's face. The entire area that had been covered by the mask was coated by the white dust. The camera showed that his nostrils and his mouth had been penetrated by the white dust. The dust particles were measured and found to be around 40 micrometers in diameter. The particles that penetrated the mask were the same diameter.

Covid-19 virus molecules are about 0.1 micrometers in diameter. That is 400 times smaller than the plaster particles that penetrated the mask.

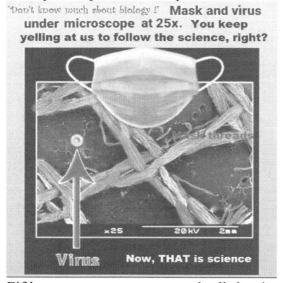

"Don't know much about biology !" **Mask and virus under microscope at 25x. You keep yelling at us to follow the science, right?**

Virus   Now, THAT is science

Fifth, no one can wear a mask all the time, such as when eating. Airlines and airports insist on extreme precautions. But on passenger airplanes and inside airports, masks are not required while eating or drinking, because it would be impossible.

There was a scandal news story when a photograph circulated of Senator Ted Cruz not wearing a mask on an airplane. The photograph was taken or at least distributed by a Hosseh who works with the Democrat Congressional Campaign Committee. [209] But soon – ooops – the obvious reality came forward that Cruz was drinking coffee. You cannot drink anything through a mask. And if you tried, the mask would be ruined. It would cease to have any effectiveness at all.

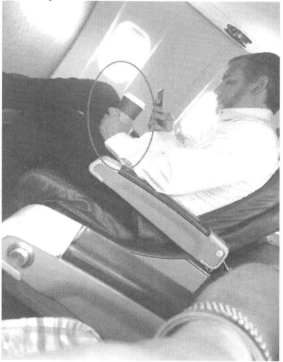

Should a national public health strategy encourage people to wear masks when they are unable to engage in social distancing? Possibly.

Should everyone be required to wear masks everywhere, regardless of local condition? Maybe.

But is it so self-evident and obvious that this is the one and only correct solution that a responsible President "must" choose those proposals? No. Not remotely.

There are significant differences of opinion about whether a strategy of voluntary use of face masks when social distancing is not possible, mandatory use of face masks when local or regional conditions require it, or a uniform nationwide requirement is the best solution or even an effective solution.

Worst of all, the experts now promoting the use of face masks were the ones telling us not to earlier in the year. So what would a competent and assertive President do? It is not so clear what "the" one and only answer should be.

However, the guidance on masks – after it flipped from telling people don't – was to wear masks *only* when social distancing was not possible.

The guidance was never "wear masks all the time." The experts told us to wear masks when social distancing was not practical.

Finally, Dr. Anthony Fauci savages "studies" that are anectodal. Well that depends on whether the study suits Fauci's agenda or not.

What is the science behind wearing masks? Exactly the kind of "observational study" with no randomized samples or scientific controls that Dr. Fauci attacks (when it suits him). So by Dr. Fauci's standards, the anectodal studies on wearing masks don't make the grade. As *The Lancet* [210] reported.

> Our search identified 172 observational studies across 16

countries and six continents, with no
randomised controlled trials and 44
relevant comparative studies in healthcare and non-health-care settings
(n=25 697 patients).

Now, this sounds very impressive until we recall
that this and all other studies on wearing masks for
COVID-19 are exactly the kind of studies that St.
Fauci tells us are an affront to science and abhorrent
and should be trampled under foot with extreme
prejudice. There are no randomized samples or
controls. No double-blind studies. Nothing that
Fauci says is essential before he would ever wound
his sainted eyes by gazing upon a study. Just a
bunch of anecdotes. Stories. What Fauci tells us
not to listen to.

MEDICAL SUPPLIES AND PERSONAL PROTECTIVE EQUIPMENT: A DISASTER OF GLOBALIST DEPENDENCE ON CHINA

Trump is criticized about the availability of Personal Protective Equipment (PPE), ventilators, and other medical equipment.

However, this actually proved Trump's warnings to be correct, that the U.S.A. was too dependent upon manufacturing that had been transferred to China from the once-prosperous U.S.A. by globalist past presidents. That's why we had shortages crippling the U.S. response.

One ingredient of this crisis was that our entire health care system was in jeopardy with China's factories and cities on lockdown. [211]

Strangely, China held nationwide New Years' celebrations up through January 21, then went into severe lockdowns, even welding shut the gates to residential complexes and shutting down factories.

As soon as China admitted the severity of the epidemic within China January 21, after New Years' celebrations, China suddenly needed all of their own factory production of PPE to fight the outbreak within China.

In fact, yes, the Trump Administration did send some of our U.S. PPE and supplies to Wuhan hoping to nip the outbreak in the bud. That was a wise strategic move. If the SARS-CoV-2 virus had been contained in Hubei Province, as happened with Ebola in one region of Africa, it would have been applauded as a master stroke. But 5 million Chinese left Hubei Province as the epidemic was spreading, transporting the virus to Italy and Iran.

Meanwhile, the factories' workers were suddenly all in quarantine at home. So the Chinese factories on which the U.S.A. depended on for importing PPEs and other medical supplies were (a) largely shut down and (b) supplying China's own emergency needs in China.

The U.S.A. made itself so dependent upon manufacturing in China that the U.S. could not function if China stopped supplying medicines, medicinal ingredients, medical equipment, and supplies. An astounding 85% of the active ingredients in pharmaceuticals in our prescription drugs are manufactured in China. *Id.*

As China's workers were ordered to stay home and not go to work in late January, U.S. efforts were hindered. China's 1.47 billion people would need those medical supplies at home. [212] China could no longer export factory output to the U.S.A.

The CDC Director testified on February 27, 2020, to the same effect. [213]

> "Many active pharmaceutical ingredients and medical supplies, including auxiliary supplies such as syringes and gloves, come from China and India."

Trump ran for President warning that the U.S. economy had sent manufacturing jobs overseas, especially to China. "We did this to ourselves," President Donald Trump keeps reminding us. China took advantage of the U.S. But we eagerly let them, guided by foolish theories and political agendas.

Yet the very same Never Trumpers, Democrats, and Leftists who set up this chronic dependence on overseas factories and attacked Trump for trying to bring those jobs home now try to smear Trump for not delivering more medical equipment and supplies.

Furthermore, these are hospital supplies for privately-owned and operated hospitals and local city government hospitals. It isn't the president's role to be the order clerk for cities and states and private hospitals. The national stockpile is for the U.S. military, the Federal Emergency Management Agency, and other U.S. federal government operations. It is not a gimme pile for private companies and city hospitals. We don't supply sheets, pillows, or medications to private hospitals.

So private and city-owned hospitals were responsible to order their own supplies, which under normal conditions would be very cheap and easy to do. Having an adequate supply of N-95 masks would be inexpensive and effortless with China's factories operating normally.

Nevertheless, the Trump Administration, federal agencies, COVID-19 Task Force, and State Governors moved heaven and Earth to solve the shortfall of medical supplies and personal protective equipment.

Critics accuse Trump of failing to invoke the "Defense Production Act" **50 USC Ch. 55.** for the purpose of mandating that U.S. factories produce supplies needed for responding to the pandemic.

Yet another lie.

Paper orders do not change the laws of physics. Factories do not shift to producing a completely different product – especially passing quality controls – just because a piece of paper orders them to do so. For a factory to stop producing one product, create a whole new assembly line, arrange for suppliers to bring all the parts together in the same place in the right quantity, order related manufacturing materials, chemicals, tools, etc., create the dies and machinery that produces parts, then plan out the assembly process, perform testing and quality checks, train workers, and then test the result, normally takes months if not years. The goal is not to throw together junk that merely looks like the desired product, but to ensure reliable, consistent, high quality, especially with a disease.

Now, critics have answered that making hospital gowns and the simple blue cloth masks does not take much time to change the assembly lines. But who cares? Disposable, paper gowns were not the problem. Anyone can make throw-away gowns, and they were not an issue – unless a hospital was just stingy and cheap in buying them.

Similarly, the simple blue rectangle masks were not the problem. But those are not N-95 masks, which were a problem. N-95 masks are specialized artificial fabric molded together in five layers.

Throughout March, 2020, President Trump was holding the powers of the Defense Production Act over suppliers negotiate and work with them on a voluntary basis to get the job done.

But issuing orders does not make PPE or medical devices magically appear. The factories have to cooperate and work overtime and triple shifts to voluntarily cooperate. And they did, eagerly.

Trump did not need the DPA until certain companies like 3M and General Motors were exporting PPE and medical device production to other countries instead of selling them here at home.

I would guess that these companies were honoring existing contracts with other countries, and the DPA gave them legal cover to break those international contracts. But Trump's anger suggests that it was worse non-cooperation. See Trump's tweet on March 27, 2020. [214]

Reported on April 4, 2020 from April 3, Trump transitioned from using the DPA as a threat to actually mandate production of PPE and medical devices. [215]

> Details: The president's memo on Friday directs the Secretary of Homeland Security and FEMA administrator to use "all authority available" under the Defense Production Act "to allocate to domestic use, as appropriate," N-95 respirators, PPE surgical masks, PPE gloves and other face respirators.

However, the reason for using the DPA was not to get factories to magically shift their production to PPE and ventilators. It was to prevent profiteering and the export of these products to other countries. Most companies were cooperating voluntarily as fast they could.

On April 2, 2004, Trump invoked the DPA: [216]

> President Donald Trump on Thursday invoked the Defense Production Act to push 3M and six major medical device companies to produce protective masks and ventilators needed for the coronavirus outbreak, bowing to weeks of pressure to expand the federal government's use of the emergency statute.
>
> "Moments ago, I directed Secretary Azar and acting Secretary Wolf to use

any and all available authority under the Defense Protection Act to ensure that domestic manufacturers have the supplies they need to produce ventilators for patients with severe cases of Covid-19," Trump said at his Thursday press conference.

The medical device DPA order covers General Electric, Hill-Rom Holdings, Medtronic, ResMed, Phillips and Vyaire Medical, authorizing HHS Secretary Alex Azar to "facilitate the supply of materials to the [companies] for the production of ventilators," according to a White House statement.

Trump said the order will help the companies "overcome obstacles of the supply chain that threaten the rapid supply of ventilators."

A Medtronic spokesperson said the company is still reviewing the medical device order, but its preliminary understanding is that the administration "is working to ensure that ventilator manufacturers, such as Medtronic, have the necessary supplies we need to continue to increase our production of these critical products."

As New York Governor Andrew Cuomo explained on April 6, 2020, in a nationally televised press conference, including on CNBC:

So when anyone needs anything we're there. Right now healthcare wide. I am going to get on the phone with the hospitals now. There is no hospital that needs ventilators that does not have ventilators. There is no hospital that needs PPE that doesn't have it... within the state system. Again, they are all going to say they are running low, because they are. But nobody who doesn't have what they need to do their job. And that's my point on perspective. Are we managing this situation the best that it can be managed? Yes. Have we lost anyone we could have saved? I don't think so. [217]

TRUMP'S "SLOW" TESTING EFFORTS?

Trump's attackers blame him for not getting widespread testing for the Wuhan virus up and running earlier. They are wrong.

As of this update, over 79 million Americans have been tested for COVID-19. That is 20% of the population. That is more people who have been tested than the rest of the world's testing combined.

First, the blame-storming often implies, curiously, that a test cures people. That's the way they talk about testing. And remember: The criticism of testing was in the time period of January through May. Since then testing has become a major success of the Trump Administration.

Because there were no proven treatments that early, knowing that someone tested positive for COVID-19 would not help in treating them. If there were a treatment, then a person who tested positive would be given an appropriate treatment.

Now, as of today of this writing in August 2020, that has changed. By June or July, there started to be treatments emerging like Remdesivir and convalescent plasma.

Trump's critics reject the use of hydroxychloroquine even though many nations have been using it to treat malaria since 1955. Eventually, many nations in Africa and around the world are going to fully test the drug whether Dr. Anthony Fauci tries to talk them out of it or not. I could easily write a book about this, but I am avoiding the topic to get these details out quickly and to avoid being banned and censored. However, it is curious that medical scientists are baffled by the very low incidence of COVID-19 on the continent of Africa, which they cannot understand (yet).

Testing is good, but it is not a treatment or cure. The news media showed a Skype video of a woman in tears, terrified, hysterical, because she could not get tested, as if the test would treat her symptoms. There were then no treatments that could be employed if the test came back positive (to the bad).

Second, the Trump Administration moved quickly and effectively, has led the world in testing, and avoided blind alleys of defective test designs. We cannot just talk about "a test" as if anything one throws together necessarily works. There are many test designs, and some are more reliable than others. Tests for the same virus can be very different.

A test cannot be created without complete and high-quality live samples. Creating a test is not automatic, but a completely creative invention. Developing a test is hit or miss.

On January 11, 2020, China posted a pneumonia outbreak update, [218] which *lowered* the number of cases to only 41 from 59 and reported only one (1) death in China.

China's update also released the genetic sequence of the novel coronavirus. But that was just drawings on paper.

Researchers went to work. But they needed actual live samples to experiment on. Not only is a drawing inadequate to invent a test, but a test cannot be properly validated using only paper drawings. The test has to be checked with the actual, live virus.

Commissioner of the Food and Drug Administration (one agency that oversees the quality of diagnostic medical tests) Dr. Scott

Gottlieb explained "China didn't share the viral strains and the WHO should have made them do that," on Face the Nation on April 12. "Had they shared those early on, we could have developed a diagnostic test earlier, validated earlier." [219]

Tests cannot be developed before a new disease appears. The purpose is to register a positive only for the new virus but no other. Imagine a COVID-19 test that also responded to SARS, MERS, Swine Flu, N1H1, and earlier types of coronaviruses. That would tell you that you have *something* – but not specifically what you do have.

Yet haters attack Trump as if Trump should have had already sitting on the shelf test designs, kits, and inventory before the Wuhan virus was even discovered. There is no guarantee when a new virus arrives that a test will ever be invented … or when. You can't just have a test because you want one. It requires as much luck as skill to invent a new test.

As a result, when China offered early testing kits to several countries, the tests had an 80% error rate. [220]

When the CDC developed tests here in the U.S., they also did not work. [221] There is great controversy that the U.S. was slow. But that was because early test designs did not work. CDC scientists had to go back to the drawing board. But how is that Trump's fault?

As *The New York Times* reported, on February 26, 2020:

> "The C.D.C. developed a diagnostic test and distributed testing kits to local health departments around the country. But the kits were flawed, and the agency must manufacture new ones. Although a dozen states are

capable of testing for coronavirus infection, confirmatory tests must still be done by the C.D.C., a process that can take days." [222]

Creating a test that is reliable and works is a scientific discovery, not just like building a toaster. The medical researchers and scientists got it wrong. Tests developed in China and in Europe did not work. The first U.S. test development did not work. Had the first test worked, the progress of testing would have been very different. But the scientists did their best. And they struck out. It happens. Seriously, this is not a process of not screwing in a light bulb but of inventing the light bulb.

Now, how is that President Trump's fault? Even the people designing, manufacturing, and sending out the tests across the country thought the tests were going to work. So their reports up the line to the President of the United States would let him and all other government leaders believe that the testing program was on track.

Now Trump's leadership skills have resulted in 70 million Americans being tested – more than all other nations combined. [223] The United States is detecting people infected with or exposed to the virus at far greater numbers because we have tested vastly more people than any other nation on Earth.

In fact, we cannot compare the spread of COVID-19 in the United States to other countries because their measurement systems (testing) are so minimal while our country's testing is now so extensive. Other countries only seem to have fewer cases because their cases are mostly being missed, undetected.

So what can Trump critics say about Trump's tremendous testing success of reaching 70 million people in the United States? Do they congratulate the President, his Administration, and the hard-working, unsung doctors, medical researchers, scientists, lab technicians and other manufacturers of the testing and other medical wonders? Nah.

The same Trump critics who said Trump was moving too slowly are now attacking Trump for moving too quickly. Critics say that Trump rushed the tests at the expense of reliability. [224] Trump is damned for being both too slow and too fast simultaneously. Democrats in Congress want to hold oversight hearings accusing Trump of rushing COVID-19 tests into service.

NO USA DID NOT REFUSE TESTS FROM THE WORLD HEALTH ORGANIZATION

The United States never refused test kits for COVID-19 from the World Health Organization.

W.H.O. released *designs* for tests. And they helped poorer, less-developed countries not able to create their own tests.

But the *designs* that W.H.O. offered were *inferior* to those being developed by the United States and major countries in Europe. There was no reason for the U.S.A. to use W.H.O.'s design because W.H.O.'s design was of lower quality. U.S. public health officials based on past experience did not have any confidence that W.H.O. would come up with a test design any better than what the U.S.A. could design and develop in its own. (Note that by this time even though China never shared a live virus sample, only paperwork about the virus, the CDC started to have available – sadly – actual human patients carrying the actual viral infection to use in developing a U.S.-based test.)

Note that one of the mistakes in this discussion is the false assumption or implication that a test is a test. Any test will do. That's not true. A test is a scientific invention from scratch. Not all designs are equal. As noted, China's test sent to countries in Eastern Europe had an 80% error rate.

The World Health Organization has admitted that they never offered any tests for the coronavirus to the United States.

Even CNN reported that claims that the World Health Organization offered tests to the U.S.A. were false: "No discussions occurred between WHO and the CDC about providing tests to the United States, WHO spokesperson Tarik Jasarevic told CNN on Tuesday, and WHO did not offer coronavirus tests to the CDC. The United States, Jasarevic confirmed, doesn't ordinarily rely on WHO for tests because the US typically has the capacity to manufacture its own diagnostics." [225]

It is true that the test designed and manufactured by the Centers for Disease Control and Prevention had a *manufacturing* flaw as well. It took a few weeks for the U.S. test kits to be corrected and made to function reliably. But the U.S. design was still superior to what W.H.O. published as a suggestion.

Even POLITIFACT explained and ruled in "Biden falsely says Trump administration rejected WHO coronavirus test kits (that were never offered)" that -- [226]

That's Not How It Works

While it might seem odd that the Trump administration shunned the WHO's coronavirus test protocol, it's normal for countries with advanced research capabilities to want to develop a measure they trust.

"I don't know if WHO agreed to sell the kits to us, but it should never have been something we needed to do given our technological expertise and the fact we would have 'taken kits from low- and middle-income countries' that otherwise could not make or afford them," said Michael Osterholm, director of the Center for Infectious Disease Research and Policy at the University of Minnesota, in an email.

It's also unlikely, Mores said, that the WHO offered to sell kits to the U.S., because that's not normally what the organization does.

"In my experience, this is never something that I would have to purchase," he said.

Typically, Mores said, American labs have all of the basic ingredients and equipment to run the test — all that would be needed is the viral sequences and an exact testing protocol. The only catch at the moment is that supplies of those basic ingredients are stretched thin due to high demand.

Our Ruling

Biden said, "The World Health Organization offered the testing kits that they have available and to give it to us now. We refused them. We did not want to buy them."

Biden has a point that the U.S. did not attempt to use the WHO test. But the U.S. would never have needed complete kits from WHO. Even if it had adopted the WHO testing approach, it already had access to all the necessary materials.

> WHO said there was never any talk of
> WHO sending testing kits to the
> United States.
>
> Biden's words leave out other
> important context and information.
>
> The U.S. chose to use its own test,
> rather than the one circulated by
> WHO. Other nations, such as China,
> Japan and France, also developed their
> own tests. Multiple public health
> experts said that is not unusual.
>
> Biden's emphasis on WHO offering
> kits is simply wrong.
>
> We rate this claim Mostly False.

The United States of America was never offered tests for COVID-19. The World Health Organization published their design – that is a paper document published on the internet. So, the *design* was offered to the world.

But the implication is that W.H.O. was offering actual, physical, manufactured tests kits to the United States. To the extent that W.H.O. does that sort of thing, it arranges actual test kits only for poor, under-developed nations that do not have the capability to manufacture their own tests.

As reported in *The Hill*,[227] the Trump Administration explained that W.H.O. never offered the U.S.A. any tests, in part because W.H.O. doesn't provide tests to countries that can develop their own tests, and the U.S. Government wanted to develop its own test to ensure the highest quality, up to U.S. standards. However, manufacturing flaws and mistakes were responsible for delaying the roll-out of the new U.S. tests.

> "'No one ever offered a test that we refused,' said Adm. Brett Giroir, assistant secretary for health at the Department of Health and Human Services. 'This was a research-grade test that was not approved, not submitted to the FDA [Food and Drug Administration] ... there was a small number that we have greatly surpassed in a very short period of time.'"

> "The WHO test, which adopted a German test as its model, was developed soon after Chinese researchers publicly posted the genome of the coronavirus in January. It shipped millions of tests to countries around the world, but generally only those without the capability to develop their own."

> "The U.S. developed its own test around the same time, but manufacturing and quality control issues soon set it well behind the WHO."

> "CDC officials acknowledged that one of the three components of the initial test were faulty, but it took weeks before the agency approved a workaround."

"Public health experts and some governors have also said bureaucratic red tape around approvals slowed the development of new tests in the U.S."

"Administration health officials have been loosening regulations, and on Monday night the FDA said it would allow states to take responsibility for tests developed and used by laboratories in their states, without involving the federal government."

"Deborah Birx, a State Department official coordinating the White House coronavirus task force, told reporters that the testing delays were due to the rigorous scientific process involved in approving U.S. diagnostic tests."

"'We were adamant about having a high quality test based on our commercial vendors,' Birx said. 'Over the next few months you'll begin to see that other tests that were utilized around the world were not of the same quality, resulting in false positives and potentially false negatives.'"

COVID-19 IS MOSTLY A DEMOCRAT PROBLEM, NOT TRUMP'S FAULT

If Trump's failure as the nation's leader were causing the coronavirus pandemic to be worse than necessary, then why were the results so drastically different between Democrat-run States and Republican-run States – especially at first?

Now, hold on a minute. Hold your horses. Some may say that this isn't fair. Well, it is exactly what Trump's critics are saying: Trump must have done a bad job managing the disease, simply because there is a disease spreading.

So is it true that President Trump did not handle the pandemic well? If we are going to analyze that argument and break it down, we run into the reality that – especially at the first (very dramatically) the problem was distinctly different in some States compared to others. The attacks do not make sense.

The pandemic is not driven by national policies. If Trump's supposed mistakes were to blame, the problem would be evenly-distributed nationally.

President Trump's leadership response to the virus is nationwide. So why have the problems with the coronavirus been so radically different in different parts of the country? The problem with the virus has been a localized phenomenon, highly dependent upon localized leadership in each State or major city.

Trump's critics argue that merely because Trump is President, therefore he is automatically to blame for anything the virus did anywhere in the nation.

So why wouldn't that same logic apply to the States run by Democrats like New York and New Jersey? If the premise of their argument were true, wouldn't the Governor of each State be "to blame" and responsible for the disease epidemic in each state?

If Trump's national leadership were to blame, then the problems from the virus would be the same nation-wide. But it wasn't and it isn't.

Instead we had a localized disease epidemic highly concentrated in cities and states that have been dominated by Democrat party leadership for many decades, and almost no impact of the disease in other parts of the country, whether Republican dominated or mixed, without a history of Democrat party leadership.

Now, today, after many months, the virus has started to spread from the hot spots in Democrat-led cities. But where we are seeing the virus spreading throughout the country now, it very distinctly started in only certain parts of the country.

Democrat controlled states suffering COVID-19 outbreak, while Republican states doing well

Therefore, why wouldn't we analyze each State and major city the way Trump's critics want to argue about Trump's national leadership? Why would we ignore that the virus was an epidemic in certain States but not others?

Left-wing attempts to shift the blame to our President for a virus that spread from China's Hubei province are false.

Now, some of these arguments may seem strange. But if we are to compare apples to apples, oranges to oranges, we would have to use the same type of analysis that critics of Trump are using, in order to find the errors.

Should we analyze the virus' impact based on the party affiliation of the Governor and Mayor? Well, yes, if we are trying to meet the criticisms of Trump head-on. If we are trying to analyze and respond to the claim that merely because Trump is President therefore anything that any disease does in the country is Trump's fault.

Otherwise if we "correct" their reasoning, both at the same time, then we will have a harder time understanding where Trump critics go wrong. It is better to follow the same line of reasoning and show where their facts are wrong.

Then we can also, after that, challenge and examine their reasoning and view of the world as well. But let's start by analyzing the topic one step at a time.

Just seven (7) Democrat controlled States account for 51% of all deaths identified as from COVID-19 up through mid-August: Out of 214,081 deaths, New York registered 32,446 deaths, New Jersey 15,925, California 11,520, Massachusetts 8,848, Illinois 8,017, Michigan 6,607, and Louisiana 4,554. Democrat-run Louisiana is significant because it held Mardi Gras [228] on February 25. [229] The highest deaths per 100,000 population are New York, New Jersey,

Massachusetts, Connecticut, Rhode Island, and Louisiana. [230]

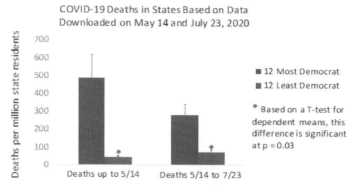

COVID-19 Deaths in States Based on Data Downloaded on May 14 and July 23, 2020

So the spread nationwide was driven largely by Democrat-run New York and New Jersey and Mardi Gras in New Orleans. [231] As of April 30, New York and New Jersey alone accounted for 40.5% of all COVID-19 cases. Adding Massachusetts and Louisiana brought just those four Democrat-run states to 49.2% of the nations' total of cases. Louisiana had 28,001 cases or another 2.7% of the national total. Massachusetts – with Boston's infamous subway system -- had 62,205 cases or another 6% of the national total.

Trump critics counter that population density is to blame. But good leadership would know their local conditions in New York and could manage their own city and state. Meanwhile, other high-density cities did not show the same explosion as New York City and the surrounding region. We did not see the same nuclear bomb of COVID-19 in Chicago, Los Angeles, San Francisco, Detroit, Atlanta, etc., although the New York epidemic has spread to those cities.

CHINA'S SUPPRESSION OF
INFORMATION HINDERED RESPONSE

The world lost one or two months in preparing a response because China censored and even destroyed information (including samples) of the COVID-19 virus.

As chronicled in The Sunday Times of the United Kingdom,

> Chinese laboratories identified a mystery virus as a highly infectious new pathogen by late December last year, but they were ordered to stop tests, destroy samples and suppress the news, a Chinese media outlet has revealed.

> A regional health official in Wuhan, centre of the outbreak, demanded the destruction of the lab samples that established the cause of unexplained viral pneumonia on January 1. China did not acknowledge there was human-to-human transmission until more than three weeks later.

> The detailed revelations by Caixin Global, a respected independent publication, provide the clearest evidence yet of the scale of the cover-up in the crucial early weeks when the opportunity was lost to control the outbreak.

Censors have been rapidly deleting the report from the Chinese internet.

Caixin reported that several genomics companies sequenced the coronavirus by December 27 from samples from patients who had fallen sick in Wuhan. [232]

China's authorities explicitly lied to the Center for Disease Control concerning crucial details showing that COVID-19 was a potential epidemic from human to human transmission:

When a CDC team was sent to Wuhan on January 8, it was deliberately not informed that medical staff had already been infected by patients — a clear confirmation that the disease was contagious.

The cover-up was led by officials in Wuhan as provincial party chiefs prepared to gather for an annual meeting. The city then pressed ahead with a pot-luck dinner for 40,000 families to celebrate the lunar new year.

Only on January 20 was it made public, in an interview with Zhong Nanshan, a respiratory health expert who led the fight against Sars, that the disease was spreading between humans.

Wuhan, with a population of 11 million, was put into lockdown on

> January 23 as the communist authorities finally tried to control the spread of the disease.

Id. [233]

Researchers at the University of Southampton, in the United Kingdom determined that: "The research also found that if interventions in the country could have been conducted one week, two weeks, or three weeks earlier, cases could have been reduced by 66 percent, 86 percent and 95 percent respectively – significantly limiting the geographical spread of the disease." [234]

> "When discussion of the outbreak began to appear online in late December, the Wuhan government moved quickly to suppress the news. Wuhan Public Security went so far as to investigate and detain eight doctors who posted on social media about the virus. Accused of spreading "illegal and false" information, the eight were made to sign a Jan. 3 letter saying that they had "severely disrupted social order." State media followed this up with reminders from the police that it would pursue anyone else who spread false rumors." [235]

> "In China's latest efforts to hide the truth about COVID-19, the communist regime has issued explicit guidance [236] to censor academic papers on the virus. By order of the government, research related to the origins of the

virus must go all the way to the top, to the central government, before researchers are permitted to submit their work for publication."

The research also found that if interventions in the country could have been conducted one week, two weeks, or three weeks earlier, cases could have been reduced by 66 percent, 86 percent and 95 percent respectively – significantly limiting the geographical spread of the disease.

A study by the University of Southampton examining non-pharmaceutical interventions (NPIs) in response to the new coronavirus (COVID-19) in China shows that a range of early, coordinated and targeted measures are needed to help significantly reduce its spread.

Researchers in the population mapping group WorldPop ran complex modelling, using anonymised data on both human movement and illness onset, to help simulate different outbreak scenarios for cities in mainland China. This allowed them to understand how variations in the timing, level and combinations of interventions affect speed and transmission of the disease.

Findings are available in a preprint paper on medRxiv website.[1] 237

The study estimates that by the end of February 2020 there was a total of 114, 325 COVID-19 cases in China. It shows that without non-pharmaceutical interventions – such as early detection, isolation of cases, travel restrictions and cordon sanitaire – the number of infected people would have been 67 times larger than that which actually occurred. [238]

As the *Times of Israel* reported: [239]

For 40 days, President Xi Jinping's CPC concealed, destroyed, falsified, and fabricated information about the rampant spread of COVID-19 through its state-sanctioned massive surveillance and suppression of data; its misrepresentation of information; its silencing and criminalizing of its dissent; and its disappearance of its whistleblowers.

In late December 2019, Dr. Ai Fen, director of the Emergency Department at the Central Hospital of Wuhan — "The Whistle-Giver" — disseminated information about COVID-19 to several doctors, one of whom was Dr. Li Wenliang, and eight of whom were later arrested. Dr. Ai has recently disappeared.

Dr. Ai also detailed efforts to silence her in a story titled, "The one who supplied the whistle," published in China's People (*Renwu*) magazine in March. The article has since been removed.

On January 1, 2020, Dr. Li Wenliang — the "hero" and "awakener" — was reprimanded for spreading rumors and was summoned to sign a statement accusing him of making false statements that disturbed the public order. Seven other people were arrested on similar charges. Their fate is still unknown.

On January 4, 2020, Dr. Ho Pak Leung — president of the University of Hong Kong's Centre for Infection — indicated that it was highly probable that COVID-19 spread from human-to-human and urged the implementation of a strict monitoring system.

For weeks, the Wuhan Municipal Health Commission declared that preliminary investigations did not show any clear evidence of human-to-human transmission.

On January 14, 2020, the WHO reaffirmed China's statement, and on January 22, 2020, Director-General Tedros Adhanom Ghebreyesus praised the CPC's handling of the outbreak, commending China's Minister of Health for his cooperation, and

> President Xi and Premier Li for their invaluable leadership and intervention.
>
> On January 23, 2020, Chinese authorities announced their first steps to quarantine Wuhan. By then, it was too late. Millions of people had already visited Wuhan and left during the Chinese New Year, and a significant number of Chinese citizens had traveled overseas as asymptomatic carriers.

Rebeccah Heinrichs, "Five lies China is telling about coronavirus," *The Washington Examiner*, April 15, 2020. [240]

China's government is still repressing the flow of information about the COVID-19 version of coronavirus, hindering the world's medical institutions and systems – including less-well-funded health systems in the so-called Third World of poorer countries less-equipped than say the United States to handle this pandemic catastrophe – from preparing and responding to this pestilence:

> In China's latest efforts to hide the truth about COVID-19, the communist regime has *issued explicit guidance* to censor academic papers on the virus. By order of the government, research related to the origins of the virus must go all the way to the top, to the central government, before researchers are permitted to submit their work for publication.

Id.

Did President Trump Save Two Million Americans?

KTLA.com said on April 13, 2020, republishing from the CNN News wire: [241]

> China has imposed restrictions on the publication of academic research on the origins of the novel coronavirus, according to a central government directive and online notices published by two Chinese universities, that have since been removed from the web.
>
> Under the new policy, all academic papers on Covid-19 will be subject to extra vetting before being submitted for publication. Studies on the origin of the virus will receive extra scrutiny and must be approved by central government officials, according to the now-deleted posts.
>
> A medical expert in Hong Kong who collaborated with mainland researchers to publish a clinical analysis of Covid-19 cases in an international medical journal said his work did not undergo such vetting in February.
>
> The increased scrutiny appears to be the latest effort by the Chinese government to control the narrative on the origins of the coronavirus pandemic, which has claimed more than 100,000 lives and sickened 1.7 million people worldwide since it first broke out in the Chinese city of Wuhan in December.

Since late January, Chinese researchers have published a series of Covid-19 studies in influential international medical journals. Some findings about early coronavirus cases — such as when human-to-human transition first appeared — have raised questions over the official government account of the outbreak and sparked controversy on Chinese social media.

And now, Chinese authorities appear to be tightening their grip on the publication of Covid-19 research.

A Chinese researcher who spoke on condition of anonymity due to fear of retaliation said the move was a worrying development that would likely obstruct important scientific research.

"I think it is a coordinated effort from (the) Chinese government to control (the) narrative and paint it as if the outbreak did not originate in China," the researcher told CNN. "And I don't think they will really tolerate any objective study to investigate the origination of this disease."

According to the directive issued by the Ministry of Education's science and technology department, "academic papers about tracing the origin of the virus must be strictly and tightly managed."

The directive lays out layers of approval for these papers, starting with the academic committees at universities. They are then required to be sent to the Education Ministry's science and technology department, which then forwards the papers to a task force under the State Council for vetting. Only after the universities hear back from the task force can the papers be submitted to journals.

Other papers on Covid-19 will be vetted by universities' academic committees, based on conditions such as the "academic value" of the study, and whether the "timing for publishing" is right.

The directive is based on instructions issued during a March 25 meeting held by the State Council's task force on the prevention and control of Covid-19, it said.

The document was first posted Friday morning on the website of the Fudan University in Shanghai, one of China's leading universities.

When CNN called a contact number left at the end of the notice, a staff member of the Education ministry's science and technology department confirmed they had issued the directive.

"It is not supposed to be made public — it is an internal document," said the person, who refused to reveal his name.

A few hours later, the Fudan University page was taken down.

The China University of Geoscience in Wuhan also posted a similar notice about the extra vetting on Covid-19 papers on its website. The page has since been deleted, but a cached version of it remains accessible.

The Chinese researcher who spoke to CNN said the notice was issued a few days ago, adding that only Covid-19 research was subject to the additional checks.

As even *The Washington Post* reported:

"While [Western] scientists and public health experts scrambled to collect more information, China's security services tried to smother it. On Jan. 1, the Wuhan Public Security Bureau summoned eight people for posting and spreading "rumors" about Wuhan hospitals receiving SARS-like cases — detentions that were reported on "Xinwen Lianbo," a newscast watched by tens of millions. ... All eight people detained that day were doctors, including Li, the Wuhan ophthalmologist." [242]

The government of China violated China's international obligations by failing to share promptly medical information about the newly and rapidly spreading viral disease. China violated China's international obligations under the convention on biological weapons to share information and affirmatively work to reduce the harm of dangerous biological agents.

China systematically deleted or erased information posted or communicated about the COIVD-19 viral outbreak. [243] China systematically, intentionally, and unlawfully withheld from the international community and medical community the information needed to fight the spread and effects of the new viral disease. [244]

China withheld critical medical information that would have dramatically improved the medical response of nations world-wide, advanced the development of a vaccine and treatments by a couple of crucial months, and slowed and lessened the spread of the viral disease before it became so widespread. [245]

Chinese authorities directed attention away from human to human infection which would have warned and informed health officials around the world and instead pointed toward the consumption of contaminated foods at the Wuhan seafood "wet market," although no actual animal was ever found as "the" point of transmission, and it has not been determined if it was a bat or some other animal. No one has found "the" animal as the culprit or smoking gun. The idea is supposition.

Yet, now, China has just re-opened the Wuhan seafood wet market. [246] China re-opening the seafood market so soon indicates that China knows that the wet market was not the cause or the source of the global pandemic.

Furthermore, around January 11 to 17: "Even after cases were being reported in Thailand and South Korea, Wuhan officials organized holiday shopping fairs like the one Pan visited. They held a downtown community potluck attended by as many as 40,000 families. They distributed hundreds of thousands of tickets to local attractions." [247]

On January 20, 2020, Wuhan celebrated the Lunar New Year with massive parades, gatherings, and parties. Across China, 400 million traveled to be with family. It was not until January 20, that renowned pulmonologist Zhong Nanshan announced on China's state media that "the virus was in fact transmissible between people." The Communist Party's official newspaper *People's Daily* mentioned the disease for the first time on January 21, 2020. China prevented Taiwan from sharing information with the World Health Organization for its political reasons. [248]

As reported by "Coronavirus and China's Missing Journalists," *National Review*, March 19, 2020: [249]

> "Three Chinese citizen journalists have gone missing in recent months. They are presumed to have been detained by Chinese authorities after posting videos on social media documenting the reality of the ongoing coronavirus pandemic."

> The most recent Chinese citizen journalist to suffer this fate was Li Zehua. Li was living a picture-perfect life. After graduating from one of

China's best universities, he began
working as a news anchor for China's
most important and prominent state
TV station, CCTV. At the age of 25,
handsome and thriving, Li was a rising
star. Had he stayed within the
boundaries the Chinese authorities
have drawn and not raised concerns
over the topics that Beijing deemed
"sensitive," he might have lived a
good, prosperous life. The coronavirus
has changed everything — at least for
Li and many like-minded young adults
in China.

As documented by a video production of
The Epoch Times, "Coronavirus – The Lies and the
Truth," by Joshua Phillips, [250] China's deceptions,
suppression of the truth about the spreading disease,
and failures recklessly spread the disease so widely
that a global pandemic became inevitable from
these early failures."Coronavirus – The Lies and the
Truth" presents these actions and omissions on a
precise timeline as a useful resource. The video has
been posted on YouTube for ease of transfer,
https://www.youtube.com/watch?v=hSIt496d82s . [251]
The Mayor of Wuhan on January 27, 2020,
as reported in this video that "He had to accept full
responsibility for what happened." *Id.* at time 3:10 –
3:50. But the Mayor of Wuhan days later explained
that that Beijing and its rules were partially
responsible for this disaster. The central
government needed to approve the release of
sensitive information about the coronavirus. *Id.* As
late as January 29, 2020, China was still arresting
citizens to prevent them from share information

about the virus with the outside world. *Id.* at time 3:50 – 4:10.

Those, including doctors and researchers, trying to spread the word in China about the new COVID-19 disease were arrested or "disappeared." Dr. Li Wenliang of Wuhan finally violated Chinese censorship and raised the alarm to the outside world internationally through a chat room of his classmates on December 30, 2019. Dr. Li was then summoned by authorities in China, reprimanded, and silenced. On February 6, 2020, Dr. Li then, not coincidentally, died of the very disease he was working to fight.

CONCLUSION

The last person anyone can blame is Donald Trump. China is the second most populated country in the world at 1.47 billion people, after India's 1.68 billion citizens. Yet many novel diseases seem to originate and spread around the world from China. China's communist government, a military coup against the government now in exile in Taiwan, is as reckless and dangerous to the world as it is to its own people.

Our President has many enemies. Those include businesses who put profits from sending U.S. manufacturing jobs to China ahead of our country's interests. They have attacked Trump to try to return our nation's policies back to favoring China from where individual companies make obscene profits at the expense of the rest of the United States. (Note it would be perfectly okay as capitalism pursuing private interest, but not when manipulating the nation's governmental foreign policy and trade policy to benefit a few against the majority. Capitalism means doing your best within the rules, rules fair to everyone, not changing the rules of the game to advantage some over others in the "game" (so to speak). Manipulating our government is different from just capitalism that I fervently support. Some call that "crony capitalism." Capitalists should win in the marketplace, not in the halls of Congress.)

It is sad and disturbing that our nation's politics are dominated so completely by lying. For decades, the rampant lying of our news media has been a chronic problem. The growing revolt of the tea party starting in 2009 and the election of Donald

Trump were reactions to many concerns, including how the political class rampantly lies to the American people.

As far back as the 1970s, the lying by the mainstream news media including CBS News was so egregious that Dana Allen and Sen. Jessie Helms launched a major campaign to buy CBS. Their campaign urged patriotic Americans to merely shift their investments, if they owned stocks and bonds, over to buying shares of CBS. Their plan did not require any new money, just shifting investments from one or several companies to CBS. As usual, conservatives and patriots didn't see the problem as all that serious and let the effort languish. Now, the news companies have changed their ownership structure to make that impossible but have gotten so much worse and done great damage.

But since the 1970s or earlier, the chronic plague of lying, deceit, and manipulation of the American people have created a strong concern of conservatives. This problem has been raging long before Donald Trump ever ran for office.

So this booklet is not just explanation. It is intended to provide you with links to hard news and facts that you can use to refute the lies with hard facts.

If you enjoy reading this booklet, that will be wonderful.

But it is my hope that some or many will go beyond that. I hope you will send a copy to your favorite local talk show / talk show host or national talk show or talk show host, your elected representatives in your State and in Congress.

I hope you will lean more heavily on the bibliography of endnotes than you do the text in the body of this booklet. I hope that you will spend more time taking the citations to the facts in the bibliography and use them to refute the lies than you do reading my opinions or explanations.

So call your local talk show and use the end notes in the bibliography to defend the truth and push back against the lies.

Write a letter to the editor. To maximize your chance of getting published, keep it short. I hate keeping things short. But it will help you get published. Re-read it several times to polish it. Then put it down for a day and pick it up fresh and read it again. Give it your best shot.

Fight back:

> "A lie is halfway around the world
> before the truth gets its boots on."

– Winston Churchill. (And others, most great quotes have been repeated by many notable figures, not just one.)

BIBLIOGRAPHY / END NOTES

[1] CNBC Television, "New York Governor Andrew Cuomo holds a news conference on the coronavirus outbreak," February 6, 2020, https://www.youtube.com/watch?v=K033NDQbC3A?t=575 at time 12:18 onward

[2] The 19 in COVID-19 refers to the year 2019 when the disease was identified.

[3] Susan Page, Mike Pence, Kamala Harris, Vice Presidential Debate, C-SPAN, October 7, 2020, starting at time 3:10, https://www.c-span.org/video/?475794-1/vice-presidential-candidates-debate

[4] Jennifer Jacobs, "White House Security Official Contracted Covid-19 in September," Bloomberg News, October 7, 2020, https://www.bloomberg.com/news/articles/2020-10-07/white-house-security-official-contracted-covid-19-in-september

[5] The Independent on YouTube, October 6, 2020, https://www.youtube.com/watch?v=09-tgDjv6Wc

[6] Darlene Superville and Aamer Madhani, "Gulf between White House's words, Trump's actions on masks," Associated Press, September 17, 2020, https://apnews.com/article/virus-outbreak-health-joe-biden-public-health-archive-41dc3fc8f146db80754c8f5b2a474c98

[7] Laura Vozzella, "Virginia Gov. Ralph Northam, wife test positive for coronavirus," The Washington Post, September 25, 2020, https://www.washingtonpost.com/local/virginia-politics/governor-northam-tests-positive-coronavirus/2020/09/25/3ae5154e-ff36-11ea-9ceb-061d646d9c67_story.html

[8] Peter Baker and Maggie Haberman, "Trump Tests Positive for the Coronavirus," *The New York Times*, October 2, 2020, https://www.nytimes.com/2020/10/02/us/politics/trump-

covid.html

[9] CNN, "Joe Biden Gives a Speech in a Delaware Corn Field; Calls Trump a "Climate Arsonist,'" September 15, 2020, https://www.youtube.com/watch?v=uvBpx7wtdrc

[10] Dr. Anthony Fauci talks with Dr Jon LaPook about Covid-19, CBS News, March 8, 2020, https://www.youtube.com/watch?v=PRa6t_e7dgI

[11] CNBC Television, "New York Governor Andrew Cuomo holds a news conference on the coronavirus outbreak," February 6, 2020, https://www.youtube.com/watch?v=K033NDQbC3A?t=575 at time 12:18 onward

[12] Justine Coleman, "Boston Globe editorial board says Trump has 'blood on his hands' over coronavirus," The Hill, April 1, 2020, https://thehill.com/homenews/media/490539-boston-globe-editorial-board-says-trump-has-blood-on-his-hands-over

[13] Valerie Richardson, "CNN quiet as Biden claims nobody would have died from virus if Trump had 'done his job,'" The Washington Times, September 18, 2020, https://www.washingtontimes.com/news/2020/sep/18/cnn-mum-biden-claims-nobody-would-have-died-if-tru/

[14] "60% of Democratic voters now blame Trump not China for coronavirus crisis: Poll," explained The Washington Times headline on April 20, 2020, https://www.washingtontimes.com/news/2020/apr/20/60-of-democratic-voters-now-blame-donald-trump-not/

[15] POLITICS: 60% of Democrats Blame Trump More Than China for Coronavirus, Monday, Rasmussen Reports, April 20, 2020, https://www.rasmussenreports.com/public_content/politics/current_events/disease/60_of_democrats_blame_trump_more_than_china_for_coronavirus

16 Reid Wilson, "Governors in all 50 states get better

marks than Trump for COVID response," The Hill, April 30, 2020, https://thehill.com/homenews/state-watch/495504-governors-in-all-50-states-get-better-marks-than-trump-for-covid

[17] "Nancy Pelosi Calls Coronavirus 'The Trump Virus,'" CNN NEWS, https://www.cnn.com/videos/politics/2020/07/21/nancy-pelosi-trump-virus-sot-blitzer-sitroom-vpx.cnn

[18] Manu Raju and Jeremy Herb, CNN, "U.S. Rep Schiff heads up '9-11 style' commission to evaluate Trump's response to COVID-19," The Atlanta Voice, April 02, 2020, https://www.theatlantavoice.com/articles/u-s-rep-schiff-heads-up-9-11-style-commission-to-evaluate-trumps-response-to-covid-19

[19] Chandelis Duster, "Pelosi on Trump's coronavirus response: 'As the President fiddles, people are dying,'" CNN, March 29, 2020, https://www.cnn.com/2020/03/29/politics/nancy-pelosi-coronavirus-cnntv/index.html

[20] Raju and Herb, endnote 18, *supra*.

[21] Mary Clare Jalonick, "Democrats proposing commission to study US pandemic response, Associated Press, April 1, 2020, https://apnews.com/5a605ec9db1e9907bc35a806cdf2a4bf

[22] Mark Simone, "Top 10 Fake News Lies About President Trump's Response to the Coronavirus, WOR 710 News Radio, April 22, 2020, https://710wor.iheart.com/featured/mark-simone/content/2020-04-21-top-10-fake-news-lies-about-president-trumps-response-to-the-coronavirus/

[23] Joe Biden's boasts about what he would have done to fight COVID-19 remind this author of his stories of his taking on "Corn Pop" at his high school's swimming pool as a teenager.

[24] David Jackson, "Trump administration declares coronavirus emergency, orders first quarantine in 50 years," USA Today, January 31, 2020, https://www.usatoday.com/story/news/politics/2020/01/31/cor onavirus-donald-trump-declares-public-health-emergency/4625299002/

[25] "Secretary Azar Declares Public Health Emergency for United States for 2019 Novel Coronavirus," Press Office, U.S. Department of Health and Human Services, January 31, 2020, https://www.hhs.gov/about/news/2020/01/31/secretary-azar-declares-public-health-emergency-us-2019-novel-coronavirus.html

[26] "US government declares the novel coronavirus a public health emergency and suspends entry for foreign nationals who visited China," CNN, January 31, 2020, https://www.cnn.com/2020/01/31/health/us-coronavirus-friday/index.html

[27] Eli Stokols, Hugo Martín, Colleen Shalby, "Trump administration declares health emergency over coronavirus; airlines cut service to China," Los Angeles Times, January 31, 2020, https://www.latimes.com/world-nation/story/2020-01-31/-health-emergency-over-coronavirus

[28] HHS, endnote 25, *supra*

[29] Allison Aubrey, "Trump Declares Coronavirus A Public Health Emergency And Restricts Travel From China," National Public Radio, January 31, 2020, https://www.npr.org/sections/health-shots/2020/01/31/801686524/trump-declares-coronavirus-a-public-health-emergency-and-restricts-travel-from-c

[30] Jessie Hellmann, "US declares public health emergency over coronavirus," The Hill, January 31, 2020, https://thehill.com/policy/healthcare/480938-us-declares-public-health-emergency-over-coronavirus

[31] Charlie Savage, "Trump Declared an Emergency Over

Coronavirus. Here's What It Can Do. The president's action will free up funds and lower legal barriers for responding to the pandemic.," The New York Times, March 13, 2020, https://www.nytimes.com/2020/03/13/us/politics/coronavirus-national-emergency.html

[32] Cleta Mitchell, "The Real Coronavirus Chronology Shows Trump Was On Top Of It While Biden Was Mocking The Danger," The Federalist, March 31, 2020, https://thefederalist.com/2020/03/31/the-real-coronavirus-chronology-shows-trump-was-on-top-of-it-while-biden-was-mocking-the-danger/

[33] Elizabeth Cohen, CNN Senior Medical Correspondent, "Vaccine for New Chinese Coronavirus in the Works," CNN News, January 20, 2020, https://www.cnn.com/2020/01/20/health/coronavirus-nih-vaccine-development/index.html

[34] "First Travel-related Case of 2019 Novel Coronavirus Detected in United States," Media Relations, Centers for Disease Control and Prevention, U.S. Department of Health and Human Services, January 21, 2020, https://www.cdc.gov/media/releases/2020/p0121-novel-coronavirus-travel-case.html

[35] "Health Alert: Restricted Travel to China due to the Coronavirus," Overseas Security Advisory Council, Bureau of Diplomatic Security, U.S. Department of State, February 3, 2020, https://www.osac.gov/Content/Report/3f2cdbc4-9672-4d33-8dad-17e0c38edfc1

[36] "Statement from the Press Secretary Regarding the President's Coronavirus Task Force, Healthcare," The white House, Executive Office of the President, January 29, 2020, https://www.whitehouse.gov/briefings-statements/statement-press-secretary-regarding-presidents-coronavirus-task-force/

[37] John Bacon, "Coronavirus: 110 people in 26 states 'under investigation' for disease; 5 U.S. cases so far," USA TODAY, January 27, 2020, updated January 29, 2020, https://www.usatoday.com/story/news/health/2020/01/27/coro

navirus-death-toll-china-wuhan-virus-outbreak-
spreads/4586403002/

[38] Julie Steenhuysen, "U.S. Announces More Coronavirus
Cases, Details Quarantine Plans for Returning Travelers,"
Reuters, FEBRUARY 3, 2020,
https://www.reuters.com/article/us-china-health-usa-cdc/us-
announces-more-coronavirus-cases-details-quarantine-plans-
for-returning-travelers-idUSKBN1ZX2F6

[39] Michael Corkery and Annie Karni, "Trump
Administration Restricts Entry Into U.S. From China," New
York Times, January 31, 2020, Updated Feb. 10, 2020,
https://www.nytimes.com/2020/01/31/business/china-travel-
coronavirus.html

[40] WCBS 880 Newsroom, "US Imposes Travel
Restrictions After Declaring Public Health Emergency Over
Coronavirus, " January 31, 2020, WCBS News Radio, January
31, 2020, https://wcbs880.radio.com/articles/news/us-
imposes-travel-restrictions-amid-public-health-emergency

[41] "CDC Issues Federal Quarantine Order to Repatriated
U.S. Citizens at March Air Reserve Base," Media Relations,
Centers for Disease Control and Prevention, U.S. Department
of Health and Human Services, January 31, 2020,
https://www.cdc.gov/media/releases/2020/s0131-federal-
quarantine-march-air-reserve-base.html

[42] Erika Edwards, "Thousands of Americans voluntarily
self-quarantine after returning from China," NBC News, Feb.
19, 2020, https://www.nbcnews.com/health/health-
news/thousands-americans-voluntarily-self-quarantine-after-
returning-china-n1138731 ; see also remarks near the end of
extensive 45 minute press conference in endnote 109, *infra.*

[43] Determination of a Public Health Emergency and
Declaration That Circumstances Exist Justifying
Authorizations Pursuant To Section 564(B) Of The Federal
Food, Drug, and Cosmetic Act, 21 U.S.C. § 360bbb-3, Office
of the Secretary, U.S Department of Health and Human
Services, February 4, 2020,

https://www.fda.gov/media/135010/download

[44] Remarks by President Trump in State of the Union Address, The White House, February 4, 2020, https://www.whitehouse.gov/briefings-statements/remarks-president-trump-state-union-address-3/

[45] Nicole Westman, "FDA issues emergency approval for coronavirus diagnostic test," The Verge, February 5, 2020, https://www.theverge.com/2020/2/5/21124005/fda-emergency-approval-coronavirus-test-cdc-diagnostic-health-labs

[46] "China's COVID-19 virus cases fall again, deaths now exceed 1,100," NBC News channel 12, Richmond, Virginia, February 11, 2020 at 3:33 AM EST - Updated February 12, https://www.nbc12.com/2020/02/11/first-new-virus-case-found-among-us-evacuees-china-quarantine-ends-some/

[47] Rebecca Falconer, "Trump administration asks Congress for $2.5 billion to fight coronavirus," AXIOS, February 25, 2020, https://www.axios.com/coronavirus-trump-congress-coronavirus-request-c7ed2f68-1dd9-468c-8f9a-b5bfe7510b3a.html

[48] Letter from Russell T. Vought Acting Director, Office of Management and Budget to Task Force leader Michael Pence and copied to Members of Congress, February 24, 2020, https://www.whitehouse.gov/wp-content/uploads/2020/02/Coronavirus-Supplemental-Request-Letter-Final.pdf

[49] Dr. Robert R. Redfield, M.D., "Testimony: House Foreign Affairs Subcommittee on Asia, the Pacific, and Nonproliferation, Coronavirus Disease 2019: The U.S. and International Response," Media Relations, Centers for Disease Control and Prevention, U.S. Department of Health and Human Services, February 27, 2020, https://www.cdc.gov/washington/testimony/2020/t20200127.htm

[50] *Ibid.*, Redfield testimony, endnote 49.

[51] "Trump Calls for Calm on Virus and Expands Travel Restrictions: The announcement included elevated warnings against travel to specific regions in Italy and South Korea, and came after the U.S. recorded its first coronavirus death: a person near Seattle," New York Times, February 29, 2020, Updated March 17, 2020, https://www.nytimes.com/2020/02/29/world/coronavirus-news.html

[52] Norimitsu Onishi, "Chaos in Europe, and Anger, Over U.S. Travel Ban to Curb Coronavirus: European leaders denounced President Trump's decision to block most visitors from the Continent for 30 days. Travelers scrambled to reach the United States before the ban takes effect," New York Times, March 12, 2020, updated July 14, 2020, https://www.nytimes.com/2020/03/12/world/europe/europe-coronavirus-travel-ban.html

[53] President Donald J. Trump, "Proclamation on Declaring a National Emergency Concerning the Novel Coronavirus Disease (COVID-19) Outbreak," The White House, Executive Office of the President, March 13, 2020, https://www.whitehouse.gov/presidential-actions/proclamation-declaring-national-emergency-concerning-novel-coronavirus-disease-covid-19-outbreak/

[54] Jan Wolfe, "Explainer: Here's what Trump's Declaration of Coronavirus Emergency Means," Reuters, March 13, 2020, https://www.reuters.com/article/us-health-coronavirus-usa-emergency-expl/explainer-heres-what-trumps-declaration-of-coronavirus-emergency-means-idUSKBN21034K

[55]Ian Schwartz, "Dr. Anthony Fauci: Travel Ban To China Absolutely Made A Difference," Real Clear Politics, March 12, 2020, https://www.realclearpolitics.com/video/2020/03/12/dr_anthony_fauci_travel_ban_to_china_absolutely_made_a_difference.html

[56] Press Release, "CMS Takes Action Nationwide to

Aggressively Respond to Coronavirus National Emergency," Newsroom, U.S. Centers for Medicare & Medicaid Services, U.S. Department of Health and Human Services, March 13, 2020, https://www.cms.gov/newsroom/press-releases/cms-takes-action-nationwide-aggressively-respond-coronavirus-national-emergency

[57] "Gatherings Should Be Limited to 10 People, Trump Says: President Trump recommended strict new guidelines, but they fell short of what experts wanted. France and the San Francisco Bay Area are ordering residents to stay home as much as possible," New York Times, March 16, 2020, updated May 6, 2020, https://www.nytimes.com/2020/03/16/world/live-coronavirus-news-updates.html

[58] The President's Coronavirus Guidelines for America, "30 Days to Slow the Spread," Coronavirus.gov, The White House, Executive Office of the President, March 16, 2020, https://www.whitehouse.gov/wpcontent/uploads/2020/03/03.16.20_coronavirus-guidance_8.5x11_315PM.pdf

[59] Nolan D. Mccaskill, Joanne Kenen and Adam Cancryn, "'This is a very bad one': Trump issues new guidelines to stem coronavirus spread," Politico, March 16, 2020, https://www.politico.com/news/2020/03/16/trump-recommends-avoiding-gatherings-of-more-than-10-people-132323

[60] Coronavirus In New Jersey: Gov. Murphy Closing All Schools, Casinos, Restaurants As COVID-19 Cases Jump To 178, CBS News Channel 3 Philly, March 16, 2020, https://philadelphia.cbslocal.com/2020/03/16/coronavirus-in-new-jersey-state-closing-casinos-restaurants-movie-theaters-amid-coronavirus-outbreak/

[61] Lisa Mascaro and Zeke Miller, "Trump pushes for massive aid from Congress, checks to public," Associated Press, March 17, 2020, https://apnews.com/22b4db74a897c8803d228269827d8612

[62] Tim Hains, "N.Y. Gov. Cuomo: President Trump Is "Fully Engaged" On Coronavirus Crisis; 'Very Creative And

Energetic,'" Real Clear Politics, March 18, 2020,
https://www.realclearpolitics.com/video/2020/03/18/ny_gov_c
uomo_president_trump_is_fully_engaged_on_coronavirus_cri
sis_very_creative_and_energetic.html

[63] Lara Seligman, "Trump deploying hospital ships to
coronavirus hot zones," POLITICO, March 18, 2020,
https://www.politico.com/news/2020/03/18/trump-navy-ship-
coronavirus-new-york-harbor-135732

[64] See Redfield testimony, endnote 49, *supra.*

[65] Katie Zezima and Rick Noack, "Trump, Trudeau agree
to close U.S.-Canada border to 'nonessential' traffic, The
Washington Post, March 18, 2020,
https://www.washingtonpost.com/world/the_americas/trump-
trudeau-us-canada-border-coronavirus/2020/03/18/90a27da8-
6924-11ea-b199-3a9799c54512_story.html

[66] President Donald Trump, "Executive Order on
Prioritizing and Allocating Health and Medical Resources to
Respond to the Spread of COVID-19," The White House, the
Executive Office of the President, March 18, 2020,
https://www.whitehouse.gov/presidential-actions/executive-
order-prioritizing-allocating-health-medical-resources-
respond-spread-covid-19/

[67] Ian Schwarz, "Fauci: The Response Of Trump Admin
Has Been Impressive, I Can't Imagine Anybody Could Be
Doing More," Real Clear Politics, March 23, 2020,
https://www.realclearpolitics.com/video/2020/03/23/fauci_the
_response_of_trump_admin_has_been_impressive_i_cant_im
agine_anybody_could_be_doing_more.html

[68] "Coronavirus Latest: Lakewood Police Charge
Homeowner For Hosting Pop-up Wedding With More Than
50 People," CBS News Channel 3 Philly, March 20, 2020,
https://philadelphia.cbslocal.com/2020/03/20/coronavirus-
latest-lakewood-police-charge-homeowner-for-hosting-pop-
up-wedding-with-more-than-50-people/

[69] C. Todd Lopez, "Corps of Engineers Converts NYC's

Javits Center Into Hospital," DOD News, U.S. Department of Defense, April 1, 2020, https://www.defense.gov/Explore/News/Article/Article/21335 14/corps-of-engineers-converts-nycs-javits-center-into-hospital/

[70] Dan Mangan and Will Feuer, "Trump allows coronavirus patients on Navy ship Comfort in New York after Cuomo asks," CNBC News, April 6, 2020, https://www.cnbc.com/2020/04/06/cuomo-will-ask-trump-to-allow-coronavirus-patients-on-comfort.html

[71] CNBC Television, "New York Governor Andrew Cuomo holds a news conference on the coronavirus outbreak," February 6, 2020, https://www.youtube.com/watch?v=K033NDQbC3A?t=575 at time 12:18 onward

[72] 'He Has Delivered for New York': Cuomo Praises Trump's Coronavirus Response: Andrew Cuomo went on The Howard Stern Show and had unexpected kind words for his frequent sparring partner," NBC News 4 New York, April 13, 2020, https://www.nbcnewyork.com/news/politics/he-has-delivered-for-new-york-cuomo-praises-trumps-coronavirus-response/2371465/

[73] "Coronavirus? Trump says be a germophobe like him," Yahoo News (Agence France- Presse), February 26, 2020, https://news.yahoo.com/coronavirus-trump-says-germophobe-him-013049352.html

[74] J. Edward Moreno, "Trump nods at reputation as germaphobe during coronavirus briefing: 'I try to bail out as much as possible' after sneezes," The Hill, February 25, 2020, https://thehill.com/homenews/administration/484875-trump-nods-at-reputation-as-germaphobe-during-coronavirus-briefing-i

[75] Daniel Lippman, "The Purell presidency: Trump aides learn the president's real red line," *The Politico*, July 7, 2019, https://www.politico.com/story/2019/07/07/donald-trump-germaphobe-1399258.

[76] Michael Crowley, "Some Experts Worry as a Germ-Phobic Trump Confronts a Growing Epidemic," New York Times, February 10, 2020, https://www.nytimes.com/2020/02/10/us/politics/trump-coronavirus-epidemic.html

[77] Donald J. Trump, @RealDonaldTrump, Twitter, https://twitter.com/realDonaldTrump/status/527529637157810176

[78] Benedict Carey and James Glanz, "Travel From New York City Seeded Wave of U.S. Outbreaks: The coronavirus outbreak in New York City became the primary source of infections around the United States, researchers have found," New York Times, May 7, 2020, updated July 16, 2020, https://www.nytimes.com/2020/05/07/us/new-york-city-coronavirus-outbreak.html

[79] "Coronavirus spread by fluids" says Mayor Deblasio, WINS News Radio, March 13, 2016, https://1010wins.radio.com/articles/news/de-blasio-says-coronavirus-not-airborne-spread-via-fluids

[80] David Marcus, "Hey, De Blasio, Close The Freakin' New York City Schools: Keeping New York City schools open in the face of coronavirus makes a mockery of social distancing. Close the schools," The Federalist, March 15, 2020, https://thefederalist.com/2020/03/15/hey-de-blasio-close-the-freakin-new-york-city-schools/

[81] Eric Bascome, "NYC public schools remain open: Parents, teachers push for closure," SILive (Staten Island Advance), March 13, 2020, https://www.silive.com/coronavirus/2020/03/nyc-public-schools-remain-open-parents-teachers-push-for-closure.html

[82] Amanda Eisenberg and Madina Touré, " De Blasio: NYC schools will close as of Monday, may not reopen this year," Politico, March 15, 2020, https://www.politico.com/states/new-york/albany/story/2020/03/15/de-blasio-nyc-schools-will-close-as-of-monday-may-not-reopen-this-year-1267141

[83] Madison Dibble, "De Blasio Haunted by Weeks-Old Tweet Urging People to 'Get Out on the Town Despite Coronavirus,'" The Washington Examiner, March 25, 2020, https://www.washingtonexaminer.com/news/de-blasio-haunted-by-weeks-old-tweet-urging-people-to-get-out-on-the-town-despite-coronavirus

[84] Madison Dibble, "De Blasio haunted by weeks-old tweet urging people to 'get out on the town despite coronavirus,'" The Washington Examiner, March 25, 2020, https://www.washingtonexaminer.com/news/de-blasio-haunted-by-weeks-old-tweet-urging-people-to-get-out-on-the-town-despite-coronavirus

[85] Julia Marsh and Nolan Hicks, "De Blasio's senior staff in near revolt over his coronavirus response," New York Post, March 20, 2020, https://nypost.com/2020/03/20/de-blasios-senior-staff-in-near-revolt-over-his-coronavirus-response/

[86] Eyewitness News ABC-7 New York, August 4, 2020, https://abc7ny.com/health/nyc-health-commissioner-resigns-slams-de-blasios-covid-response/6353061/

[87] NYC Celebratory Events in Chinatown and other NYC locales, New Yorkled Magazine, https://www.newyorkled.com/nyc-chinese-lunar-new-year-events-new-york-city/

[88] Tom Elliott, Twitter, Video of press conference, https://twitter.com/tomselliott/status/1243539798008172551

[89] Susan Edelman, "Two pols urge de Blasio to oust Health Commissioner Barbot over coronavirus response," New York Post, April 4, 2020, https://nypost.com/2020/04/04/nyc-pols-urge-de-blasio-to-oust-health-commissioner-over-coronavirus-response/

[90] Ryan Saavedra, "Bill De Blasio Refused Major Efforts To Combat Coronavirus Until Aides Threatened To Quit, Report Says," Daily Wire, March 16, 2020, https://www.dailywire.com/news/bill-de-blasio-refused-major-efforts-to-combat-coronavirus-until-aides-threatened-to-quit-

report-says

[91] Bernard Condon, Jennifer Peltz and Jim Mustian, "AP count: Over 4,500 virus patients sent to NY nursing homes," Associated Press, May 22, 2020, https://apnews.com/5ebc0ad45b73a899efa81f098330204c

[92] Holmes Lybrand, "Fact checking Gov. Cuomo's false claim about Covid-positive patients and nursing homes," CNN, https://edition.cnn.com/2020/10/01/politics/andrew-cuomo-nursing-homes-fact-check/index.html

[93] Factors Associated with Nursing Home Infections and Fatalities in New York State During the COVID-19 Global Health Crisis, New York State Department of Health, July 20, 2020, revised, https://www.health.ny.gov/press/releases/2020/docs/nh_factors_report.pdf

[94] New York State Department of Health, "Advisory: Hospital Discharges and Admissions to Nursing Homes, March 25, 2020, https://skillednursingnews.com/wp-content/uploads/sites/4/2020/03/DOH_COVID19__NHAdmissionsReadmissions__032520_1585166684475_0.pdf

[95] Dr. Tedros Adhanom Ghebreyesus, "WHO Director-General's opening remarks at the media briefing on COVID-19," World Health Organization, March 11, 2020, https://www.who.int/dg/speeches/detail/who-director-general-s-opening-remarks-at-the-media-briefing-on-covid-19---11-march-2020

[96] James Gordon Meek and Lucien Bruggeman, "CDC director downplays coronavirus models, says death toll will be 'much lower' than projected: Models released last week showed the virus could kill 100,000-240,000 Americans," ABC News, April 6, 2020, https://abcnews.go.com/Health/cdc-director-downplays-coronavirus-models-death-toll-lower/story?id=70011918

[97] See Edelman, endnote 89, *supra.*

[98] Doug Gollan, "COVID-19 Travel Update: Fauci Says Cruising Is OK If You Are Healthy," FORBES, March 9, 2020, https://www.forbes.com/sites/douggollan/2020/03/09/fauci-says-cruising-is-ok-if-you-are-healthy/#32b6e31c2d4d

[99] Susan Cornwell, Nathan Layne, Confirmed coronavirus may force Americans to avoid crowds and cancel cruises; U.S. cases near 550, Reuters, March 8, 2020, https://www.reuters.com/article/us-health-coronavirus-usa/confirmed-coronavirus-may-force-americans-to-avoid-crowds-and-cancel-cruises-u-s-cases-near-550-idUSKBN20V0MK

[100] Doctors, Rothe, Schunk, Sothmann, Bretzel, Froeschl, Wallrauch, Zimmer, Thiel, Janke, Guggemos, Seilmaier, Drosten, Vollmar, Zwirglmaier, Zange, Wölfel, Hoelscher, "Transmission of 2019-nCoV Infection from an Asymptomatic Contact in Germany," The New England Journal of Medicine, January 30, 2020, https://www.nejm.org/doi/full/10.1056/NEJMc2001468

[101] Tom Elliott, Twitter, https://twitter.com/tomselliott/status/1243595921633488898

[102] Tom Elliott, Twitter, https://twitter.com/tomselliott/status/1243597923671257088

[103] Tia Ghose, "Northern California reports first case of coronavirus not tied to travel," Live Science, February 26, 2020, www.livescience.com/amp/northern-california-coronavirus-case-community-spread.html ; Press Release, "CDC Confirms Possible First Instance of COVID-19 Community Transmission in California," Office of Public Affairs, California Department of Public Health, February 26, 2020, https://www.cdph.ca.gov/Programs/OPA/Pages/NR20-006.aspx

[104] Elizabeth Tyree, "Potential coronavirus case being investigated in Southwest Virginia," ABC TV News Channel 13, Richmond, Virginia, February 26, 2002,

https://wset.com/news/local/two-potential-coronavirus-cases-being-investigated-in-virginia

[105] Eileen AJ Connelly, "Suspected coronavirus patient isolated in New Jersey hospital," New York Post, February 29, 2020, https://nypost.com/2020/02/29/suspected-coronavirus-patient-isolated-in-new-jersey-hospital/

[106] Roni Caryn Rabin, "C.D.C. Confirms First Possible Community Transmission of Coronavirus in U.S.," New York Times, February 26, 2020, https://www.nytimes.com/2020/02/26/health/coronavirus-cdc-usa.html

[107] Dakin Andone, Jamie Gumbrecht and Michael Nedelman, "First Death from Coronavirus in the United States Confirmed in Washington State," CNN News Health, February 29, 2020, https://www.cnn.com/2020/02/29/health/us-coronavirus-saturday/index.html

[108] Eileen AJ Connelly, "Suspected coronavirus patient isolated in New Jersey hospital," New York Post, February 29, 2020, https://nypost.com/2020/02/29/suspected-coronavirus-patient-isolated-in-new-jersey-hospital/

[109] Press Conference led by Secretary Alex Azar, The Department of Health and Human Services, The National Desk, Facebook, Watch Live, 45 minutes long, February 25, 2020, https://www.facebook.com/watch/live/?extid=9sjV2A9wXER QJmyt&v=569622150575091

[110] Carla K. Johnson, AP Medical Writer, "'Simply not ready': Americans told to brace for spread of new virus," WSET News, Lynchburg, Virginia, February 25th 2020, https://wset.com/news/nation-world/time-is-everything-world-braces-for-spread-of-new-virus

[111] See, Elizabeth Tyree, endnote 104, *supra*

[112] Redfield testimony, endnote 49, *supra*

[113] Press release, "Public health screening to begin at 3 U.S. airports for 2019 novel coronavirus (-2019-nCoV')," Media Relations, Centers for Disease Control and Prevention, U.S. Department of Health and Human Services, January 17, 2020, https://stacks.cdc.gov/view/cdc/84424

[114] Coronavirus: First death confirmed in Europe, BBC News, February 15, 2020, https://www.bbc.com/news/world-europe-51514837

[115] Tom Elliott, "How NYC's Political Brass Set the Stage for City Becoming America's Coronavirus Epicenter: For months city officials assured New Yorkers they should continue life as usual," Grabien News, March 28, 2020, https://news.grabien.com/story-how-nycs-trump-opposition-led-city-becoming-americas-coronav

[116] AJMC Staff, "What We're Reading: Coronavirus Deaths Exceed SARS; Trump Delays Kidney Dialysis Rule; Lost, Delayed Lifesaving Organs," The American Journal of Managed Care, February 10, 2020, https://www.ajmc.com/view/what-were-reading-coronavirus-deaths-exceed-sars-trump-delays-kidney-dialysis-rule-lost-delayed-lifesaving-organs

[117] Video of news conference aired on TV, https://www.air.tv/?v=cPM_UNf8RJ2Bz3lt5P-jAg and https://news.grabien.com/story-flashback-nyc-health-commissioner-urged-new-yorkers-gather-p

[118] Press Release, "HHS and CDC Receive Additional Flights Carrying Passengers from China," Newsroom, U.S. Centers for Medicare & Medicaid Services, U.S. Department of Health and Human Services, February 5, 2020, https://www.cdc.gov/media/releases/2020/s0205-china-passengers.html

119 Sam Pierce, Tweet of Chuck Schumer, Twitter, February 5, 2020, https://twitter.com/SamPierce65/status/1239899657054060545

[120] Tom Elliott, "Flashback: NYC 'Health Commissioner' Urged New Yorkers to Gather in Public Places 'There is no reason not to take the subway, not to take the bus, not to go out to your favorite restaurant, and certainly not to miss the parade next Sunday'", Grabien News, March 27, 2020, https://news.grabien.com/story-flashback-nyc-health-commissioner-urged-new-yorkers-gather-p

[121] See Elliott, Flashback, endnote 120, *supra*.

[122] See Elliott, Flashback, endnote 120, *supra*.

[123] AIR TV, Video montage by Grabien News, at https://www.air.tv/?v=KgXbxTw5TnydP4xVuoC3rA

[124] See Elliott, Flashback, endnote 120, *supra*.

[125] Manuela Andreoni, Los Angeles Times, March 22, 2020, https://www.latimes.com/world-nation/story/2020-03-22/last-passengers-all-americans-evacuated-from-quarantined-cruise-ship-off-brazil-coast

[126] Freida Frisaro, Adriana Gomez Licon, and The Associated Press, "Cruise ships stuck at sea 'indefinitely' with sick onboard amid coronavirus pandemic, Coast Guard says," Fortune, April 1, 2020, https://fortune.com/2020/04/01/cruise-ships-out-of-florida-coronavirus-stuck-at-sea/

[127] By Karen Leigh and Dandan Li, "China Blasts U.S. for 'Overreaction' to Virus, Spreading Fear," Bloomberg News, February 3, 2020, https://www.bloomberg.com/news/articles/2020-02-03/china-blasts-u-s-for-overreaction-to-virus-spreading-fear

[128] Press release, "HHS and CDC Receive Additional Flights Carrying Passengers from China," Media Relations, Centers for Disease Control and Prevention, U.S. Department of Health and Human Services, February 5, 2020, https://www.cdc.gov/media/releases/2020/p0130-coronavirus-spread.html

[129] Press release, "CDC Confirms Person-to-Person Spread of New Coronavirus in the United States," Media Relations, Centers for Disease Control and Prevention, U.S. Department of Health and Human Services, January 30, 2020, https://www.cdc.gov/media/releases/2020/p0130-coronavirus-spread.html

[130]   Andrew Joseph, "WHO declares coronavirus outbreak a global health emergency," STAT News, January 30, 2020, https://www.statnews.com/2020/01/30/who-declares-coronavirus-outbreak-a-global-health-emergency/

[131] Dr. Marc Siegel, M.D., "The New Coronavirus Isn't a Threat to People in the United States — But Flu Is," Los Angeles Times, January 29, 2020, https://www.latimes.com/opinion/story/2020-01-29/coronavirus-no-threat-to-americans-but-flu-is

[132] J. Edward Moreno, "Government health agency official: Coronavirus 'isn't something the American public need to worry about,'" The Hill, January 26, 2020, https://thehill.com/homenews/sunday-talk-shows/479939-government-health-agency-official-corona-virus-isnt-something-the

[133] Transcript, Emergency Committee on novel coronavirus in China, International Health Regulations, World Health Organization, 23 January 2020, https://www.who.int/docs/default-source/coronaviruse/transcripts/ihr-emergency-committee-for-pneumonia-due-to-the-novel-coronavirus-2019-ncov-press-briefing-transcript-23012020.pdf

[134] E.J. Mundell and Dennis Thompson, "First U.S. Case of China Coronavirus Diagnosed," WebMd, January 21, 2020, https://www.webmd.com/lung/news/20200121/first-us-case-of-china-coronavirus-diagnosed

[135] Greg Kelly Reports, "In January, Dr Tony Fauci was on my show telling America not to worry about the Coronavirus—that it wasn't a major threat to the people.

January 21, 2020, 20 seconds:," Twitter,
https://twitter.com/gregkellyusa/status/1246060637748330496

[136] Javier C. Hernández and Austin Ramzy, "China
Confirms New Coronavirus Spreads From Humans to
Humans," New York Times, January 20, 2020, updated
February 19, 2020,
https://www.nytimes.com/2020/01/20/world/asia/coronavirus-
china-symptoms.html

[137] AJMC Staff, "What We're Reading: Roots of Chinese
Illness Discovered; Birth Costs Soar; Public Health
Emergency in Puerto Rico," The American Journal of
Managed Care, January 9, 2020,
https://www.ajmc.com/view/what-were-reading-roots-of-
chinese-illness-discovered-birth-costs-soar-public-health-
emergency-in-puerto-rico

[138] AJMC Staff, "What We're Reading: Insurers Plan to
Manufacture Drugs; Trump Hints at Cutting Medicare; China
Quarantines Wuhan," The American Journal of Managed
Care, January 23, 2020, https://www.ajmc.com/view/a-
timeline-of-covid19-developments-in-2020

[139] Cleta Mitchell, endnote 32, *supra*.

[140] World Health Organization, "Preliminary investigations
conducted by the Chinese authorities have found no clear
evidence of human-to-human transmission of the novel
#coronavirus (2019-nCoV) identified in #Wuhan, #China,"
Twitter,
https://twitter.com/WHO/status/1217043229427761152

[141] Amy Qin and Javier C. Hernández, "China Reports
First Death From New Virus," The New York Times, January
10, 2020, updated Jan. 21, 2020,
https://www.nytimes.com/2020/01/10/world/asia/china-virus-
wuhan-death.html

[142] Helen Branswell, "WHO says mysterious illness in
China likely being caused by new virus," STAT News,
January 8, 2020, https://www.statnews.com/2020/01/08/who-
says-mysterious-illness-in-china-likely-being-caused-by-new-

virus/?

[143] Health Alert Network, "Outbreak of Pneumonia of Unknown Etiology (PUE) in Wuhan, China," Emergency Preparedness and Response, Centers for Disease Control and Prevention, U.S. Department of Health and Human Services, January 30, 2020, https://emergency.cdc.gov/han/han00424.asp

[144] Josh Margolin and James Gordon Meek, "Intelligence report warned of coronavirus crisis as early as November: Sources: 'Analysts concluded it could be a cataclysmic event, a source said,'" ABC News, April 8, 2020, https://abcnews.go.com/Politics/intelligence-report-warned-coronavirus-crisis-early-november-sources/story?id=70031273

[145] Jamie McIntyre, "Pentagon denies ABC News report that intelligence warned of 'cataclysmic' coronavirus pandemic last November," The Washington Times, April 9, 2020, https://www.washingtonexaminer.com/policy/defense-national-security/pentagon-denies-abc-news-report-that-intelligence-warned-of-cataclysmic-coronavirus-pandemic-last-november

[146] Jamie McIntyre, "Pentagon denies ABC News report that intelligence warned of 'cataclysmic' coronavirus pandemic last November," The Washington Times, April 9, 2020, https://www.washingtonexaminer.com/policy/defense-national-security/pentagon-denies-abc-news-report-that-intelligence-warned-of-cataclysmic-coronavirus-pandemic-last-november

[147] https://twitter.com/WHO/status/1217043229427761152

[148] I am tempted to include the cartoon of Alfred E. Neumann, but I don't want some bogus copyright claim to stop the publication and distribution of this important booklet.

[149] Jackson Ryan, "Coronavirus and COVID-19: All your questions answered," Cnet.com, March 11, 2020, section "Where did the virus come from," https://www.cnet.com/how-

to/coronavirus-and-covid-19-all-your-questions-
answered/#wherefrom (emphasis in original).

[150] See, also, Prof Chaolin Huang, MD, Yeming Wang,
MD, Prof Xingwang Li, MD, Prof Lili Ren, PhD, Prof
Jianping Zhao, MD, Yi Hu, MD, et al., "Clinical features of
patients infected with 2019 novel coronavirus in Wuhan,
China," THE LANCET, Volume 395, Issue 10223, February
15, 2020,
https://www.thelancet.com/journals/lancet/article/PIIS0140-
6736(20)30183-5/fulltext#seccestitle170

[151] Helen Braswell, "The months of magical thinking: As
the coronavirus swept over China, some experts were in
denial, STATE NEWS, April 20, 2020,
https://www.statnews.com/2020/04/20/the-months-of-
magical-thinking-as-the-coronavirus-swept-over-china-some-
experts-were-in-denial-about-what-was-to-come/

[152] Sheri Fink, "White House Takes New Line After Dire
Report on Death Toll: Federal guidelines warned against
gatherings of more than 10 people as a London report
predicted high fatalities in the U.S. without drastic action,"
New York Times, March 16, 2020,
https://www.nytimes.com/2020/03/16/us/coronavirus-fatality-
rate-white-house.html

[153] Nicholas Kristof, "The Best-Case Outcome for the
Coronavirus, and the Worst: Will we endure 2.2 million
deaths? Or will we manage to turn things around?" The New
York Times, March 20, 2020,
https://www.nytimes.com/2020/03/20/opinion/sunday/coronav
irus-outcomes.html

[154] David Adam, "Special report: The simulations driving
the world's response to COVID-19: How epidemiologists
rushed to model the coronavirus pandemic," Nature Magazine,
April 3, 2020, updated April 3, 2020,
https://www.nature.com/articles/d41586-020-01003-6

[155] Sharon Lerner, "2.2 Million People In The U.S. Could
Die If Coronavirus Goes Unchecked," The Intercept, March

17 2020, https://theintercept.com/2020/03/17/coronavirus-air-pollution/

[156] Neil M Ferguson, Daniel Laydon, Gemma Nedjati-Gilani et al., "Impact of non-pharmaceutical interventions (NPIs) to reduce COVID-19 mortality and healthcare demand. Imperial College London (16-03-2020)," On behalf of the Imperial College COVID-19 Response Team WHO Collaborating Centre for Infectious Disease Modelling MRC Centre for Global Infectious Disease Analysis Abdul Latif Jameel Institute for Disease and Emergency Analytics Imperial College London, https://www.imperial.ac.uk/media/imperial-college/medicine/sph/ide/gida-fellowships/Imperial-College-COVID19-NPI-modelling-16-03-2020.pdf

[157] Note that the report is from England, and the spelling of some words is from the British spelling of words. The spelling is not a mistake but is in the original report.

[158] William Wan, Lenny Bernstein, Laurie McGinley and Josh Dawsey, "Draft report predicts covid-19 cases will reach 200,000 a day by June 1," The Washington Post, May 4, 2020, https://www.washingtonpost.com/health/government-report-predicts-covid-19-cases-will-reach-200000-a-day-by-june-1/2020/05/04/02fe743e-8e27-11ea-a9c0-73b93422d691_story.html

[159] https://www.washingtonpost.com/context/draft-government-report-projecting-a-surge-of-covid-19-cases/2b35321d-3977-41f5-9a78-50da7cafbe06/?itid=lk_inline_manual_1

[160]https://www.worldometers.info/coronavirus/country/us/, accessed on October 3, 2020

[161] Remarks by President Trump in State of the Union Address, The White House, February 4, 2020, https://www.whitehouse.gov/briefings-statements/remarks-president-trump-state-union-address-3/

[162] User Clip, President Trump Campaign Event in North

Charleston, South Carolina, C-SPAN, February 28, 2020, https://www.c-span.org/video/?c4868138/user-clip-proof-donald-trump-coronavirus-hoax-dishonest-attacks-hoax

163 Bethania Palma, U.S. President Donald Trump referred to the new coronavirus as a "hoax." SNOPES, March 2, 2020, https://www.snopes.com/fact-check/trump-coronavirus-rally-remark/

164https://assets.donaldjtrump.com/2017/web/hero_images/As_filed_Complaint_against_WJFW-NBC.pdf

165 Rem Rieder, "Democratic Ad Twists Trump's 'Hoax' Comment," FACTCHECK POSTS, April 14, 2020, https://www.factcheck.org/2020/04/democratic-ad-twists-trumps-hoax-comment/

166 Rem Rieder, FACTCHECK POSTS, "Trump and the 'New Hoax,'" FactCheck.org, March 3, 2020, https://www.factcheck.org/2020/03/trump-and-the-new-hoax/?platform=hootsuite

167 Hope Yen, "AP FACT CHECK: Biden distorts Trump's words on virus 'hoax,'" Associated Press, September 17, 2020, https://apnews.com/article/election-2020-virus-outbreak-ap-fact-check-politics-joe-biden-1eea443cca46df5f18e61b7c34549da2

168   C-SPAN, https://www.c-span.org/video/?c4868138/user-clip-proof-donald-trump-coronavirus-hoax-dishonest-attacks-hoax

169 Lauren Weber, "Sudden Departure Of White House Global Health Security Head Has Experts Worried," May 9, 2018, updated May 10, 2018, https://www.huffpost.com/entry/tim-ziemer-global-health-security-leaves_n_5af37dfbe4b0859d11d02290

170 Tim Morrison, "No, the White House didn't 'dissolve' its pandemic response office. I was there.," Washington Post, March 16, 2020, https://www.washingtonpost.com/opinions/2020/03/16/no-

white-house-didnt-dissolve-its-pandemic-response-office/

[171] by the Trump Administration – author

[172] Rebeccah Heinrichs, "The Truth about the National Security Council's Pandemic Team," National Review, April 1, 2020, https://www.nationalreview.com/2020/04/coronavirus-truth-national-security-council-pandemic-team/

[173] President Trump, The White House, "Presidential Memorandum on the Support for National Biodefense," September 18, 2018, https://www.whitehouse.gov/presidential-actions/presidential-memorandum-support-national-biodefense/

[174] The White House, "National Biodefense Strategy," The Executive Office of the President, September 2018, https://www.whitehouse.gov/wp-content/uploads/2018/09/National-Biodefense-Strategy.pdf

[175] President Donald Trump, The White House, "Executive Order on Modernizing Influenza Vaccines in the United States to Promote National Security and Public Health," Executive Office of the President, September 19, 2019, https://www.whitehouse.gov/presidential-actions/executive-order-modernizing-influenza-vaccines-united-states-promote-national-security-public-health/

[176] Kate Sheehy, "China has yet to allow CDC in country to help with coronavirus," New York Post, February 3, 2020, https://nypost.com/2020/02/03/china-has-yet-to-allow-cdc-in-country-to-help-with-coronavirus/

[177] Donald G. McNeil Jr. and Zolan Kanno-Youngs, "C.D.C. and W.H.O. Offers to Help China Have Been Ignored for Weeks," New York Times, Feb. 7, 2020, https://www.nytimes.com/2020/02/07/health/cdc-coronavirus-china.html

[178] Karen DeYoung , How the Obama White House runs foreign policy, The Washington Post, August 4, 2015,

https://www.washingtonpost.com/world/national-security/how-the-obama-white-house-runs-foreign-policy/2015/08/04/2befb960-2fd7-11e5-8353-1215475949f4_story.html

[179] Collection of Emails, published in the raw by The New York Times, https://int.nyt.com/data/documenthelper/6879-2020-covid-19-red-dawn-rising/66f590d5cd41e11bea0f/optimized/full.pdf#page=1

[180] Claire Groden, "Republican Foreign Policy Experts Pen Open Letter Bashing Trump," Fortune Magazine, March 3, 2016, https://fortune.com/2016/03/03/foreign-policy-trump/

[181] WOTR Staff, "Open Letter On Donald Trump From GOP National Security Leaders," War on the Rocks, March 2, 2016, https://warontherocks.com/2016/03/open-letter-on-donald-trump-from-gop-national-security-leaders/

[182] Jeremy Herb and Manu Raju, "House of Representatives impeaches President Donald Trump," CNN, December 19, 2019, https://www.cnn.com/2019/12/18/politics/house-impeachment-vote/index.html

[183] Li Zhouli, "Senators Aren't Even Allowed to Talk During the Impeachment Trial: The strange rule that threatens lawmakers with 'imprisonment,'" VOX, January 22, 2020, https://www.vox.com/2020/1/22/21075206/impeachment-trial-senators-talking-silent-sergeant-at-arms

[184] Natasha Bertrand and Maggie Severns, "From distraction to disaster: How coronavirus crept up on Washington," POLITICO, March 30, 2020, https://www.politico.com/news/2020/03/30/how-coronavirus-shook-congress-complacency-155058

[185] Your author once went to Kenya for 2 ½ weeks on a Christian missionary short-term mission and returned after an amazing experience to find that many members of his church didn't know he had been gone.

[186]   Donald J. Trump, Tweeter, January 27, 2020,
https://twitter.com/realdonaldtrump/status/1221809170673958
913?lang=en

[187] "Remarks by President Trump in State of the Union
Address," White House, Executive Office of the President,
February 4, 2020, https://www.whitehouse.gov/briefings-
statements/remarks-president-trump-state-union-address-3/

[188] "Trump downplays coronavirus threat in U.S. while
talking up administration's response," CBS News, February
27, 2020, https://www.cbsnews.com/video/trump-downplays-
coronavirus-threat-in-america/

[189] "54 times Trump downplayed the coronavirus," May 6,
2020, https://www.washingtonpost.com/video/politics/44-
times-trump-downplayed-the-
coronavirus/2020/03/05/790f5afb-4dda-48bf-abe1-
b7d152d5138c_video.html

[190] "Trump repeatedly downplayed the virus as the US
reopened," CNN, July 28, 2020,
https://www.cnn.com/videos/politics/2020/07/28/coronavirus-
cases-united-states-trump-comments-since-reopening-orig-
me.cnn

[191] David Leonhardt, "A Complete List of Trump's
Attempts to Play Down Coronavirus: He could have taken
action. He didn't.," The New York Times, March 15, 2020,
https://www.nytimes.com/2020/03/15/opinion/trump-
coronavirus.html

[192] Jonathon Moseley, "Coronavirus Basics Too Many
People Never Learned, American Thinker, May 23, 2020,
https://www.americanthinker.com/articles/2020/05/coronaviru
s_basics_too_many_people_never_learned.html#ixzz6XFuzC
wCF

[193] Yujun Tang, Jiajia Liu, Dingyi Zhang, Zhenghao Xu,
Jinjun Ji, and Chengping Wen, "Cytokine Storm in COVID-
19: The Current Evidence and Treatment Strategies," Frontiers

in Immunology 2020; 11: 1708, Published online 2020 Jul 10. doi: 10.3389/fimmu.2020.01708, PMCID: PMC7365923, PMID: 32754163, https://www.ncbi.nlm.nih.gov/pmc/articles/PMC7365923/

[194] Sarah Bradley, "What Is a Cytokine Storm? Doctors Explain How Some COVID-19 Patients' Immune Systems Turn Deadly. The immune system is there to help us fight infection, but sometimes it wreaks more havoc than the disease itself." Health, May 01, 2020, https://www.health.com/condition/infectious-diseases/coronavirus/cytokine-storm

[195] Jimmy McCloskey, "Coronavirus expert tells people to stop panicking because 'viruses gonna virus,'" Metro UK, March 6,2020, https://metro.co.uk/2020/03/06/coronavirus-expert-tells-people-stop-panicking-viruses-gonna-virus-12359879/

[196] Erin Schumaker, "CDC and WHO offer conflicting advice on masks. An expert tells us why," ABC News, May 29, 2020, https://abcnews.go.com/Health/cdc-offer-conflicting-advice-masks-expert-tells-us/story?id=70958380

[197] Dr. Anthony Fauci talks with Dr Jon LaPook about Covid-19, CBS News, March 8, 2020, https://www.youtube.com/watch?v=PRa6t_e7dgI

[198] CDC, Twitter, https://twitter.com/CDCgov/status/1233134710638825473

[199] Use of Masks to Help Slow the Spread of COVID-19, Centers for Disease Control and Prevention, June 28, 2020, https://www.cdc.gov/coronavirus/2019-ncov/prevent-getting-sick/diy-cloth-face-coverings.html

[200] John Yoo and Emanuel S. Heller, "The constitutionality of federal mask mandates," The OCR, July 26, 2020, https://www.ocregister.com/2020/07/26/the-constitutionality-of-federal-mask-mandates/

[201] Ilya Shapiro, "The Obamacare "Tax" That Chief Justice Roberts Invented Is Still Unconstitutional," FORBES, May

12, 2014,
https://www.forbes.com/sites/ilyashapiro/2014/05/12/the-
obamacare-tax-that-chief-justice-roberts-invented-is-still-
unconstitutional/#7ef5fb4122b7

[202] Beth LeBlanc, Craig Mauger, Melissa Nann Burke,
"High court strikes down Whitmer's emergency powers; gov
vows to use other means," The Detroit News, October 2, 2020,
https://www.detroitnews.com/story/news/local/michigan/2020
/10/02/michigan-supreme-court-strikes-down-gretchen-
whitmers-emergency-powers/5863340002/

[203] Justine Coleman, "Federal judge rules Pennsylvania's
coronavirus orders are unconstitutional," The Hill, September
14, 2020, https://thehill.com/regulation/court-battles/516333-
federal-judge-rules-pennsylvanias-coronavirus-orders-are

[204] Alex Nitzberg, "South Dakota Gov. who didn't impose
COVID-19 lockdowns: 'I don't have the authority to do that,'"
Just the News, August 27, 2020,
https://justthenews.com/nation/culture/south-dakota-gov-who-
didnt-institute-covid-19-lockdowns-i-dont-have-authority-
do?fbclid=IwAR2NxeXzhW_jrEZypTK1nySUJ4wjO8HMW
FG62ewGJU1vUaIWNeME4cIIgg8

[205] https://www.meehanmd.com/blog/2020-06-12-healthy-
people-should-not-wear-face-masks/, See June 14, 2020, entry

[206] Roni Caryn Rabin, "Many in China Wear Them, but
Do Masks Block Coronavirus?" The New York Times,
January 23, 2020, updated February 29, 2020,
https://www.nytimes.com/2020/01/23/health/coronavirus-
surgical-masks.html

[207] Occupational Health and Safety Administration, last
accessed on August 27, 2020,
https://www.osha.gov/SLTC/covid-19/covid-19-
faq.html?fbclid=IwAR0lZ3TI87kL6KyLCr5mvclZXPYBvZ6
TytJhO1YbHKMiYC0geArGU8IRcxo

[208] Andrea Widburg, "The CDC Director has doubled
down on masks, but is he wrong?" The American Thinker,
September 17, 2020,

https://www.americanthinker.com/blog/2020/09/the_cdc_direc
tor_has_doubled_down_on_masks_but_is_he_wrong.html

[209] Tweet from Hosseh, Board member, Democrat
Congressional Campaign Committee Victory Committee,
https://twitter.com/hossehenad/status/1282498098858786818

[210] Derek K Chu, Elie A Akl, Stephanie Duda, Karla Solo,
Sally Yaacoub, Holger J Schünemann, on behalf of the
COVID-19 Systematic Urgent Review Group Effort (SURGE)
study authors, Funded by the World Health Organization,
Physical distancing, face masks, and eye protection to
prevent," The Lancet, June 1, 2020,
https://www.thelancet.com/journals/lancet/article/PIIS0140-
6736(20)31142-9/fulltext

[211] Caitlin Owens,"Coronavirus outbreak fuels concerns
about pharma's global supply chain," AXIOS, January 28,
2020, https://www.axios.com/coronavirus-outbreak-pharma-
supply-chain-china-5d78af7f-b688-4735-94ea-
97d0086e6513.html

[212] "Coronavirus: Virus fears trigger Shanghai face mask
shortage," BBC, January 23, 2020 ("A new virus that has
emerged in China has seen customers flocking to buy face
masks and sanitiser."),
https://www.bbc.com/news/video_and_audio/headlines/51219
365/coronavirus-virus-fears-trigger-shanghai-face-mask-
shortage/

[213] Redfield testimony, endnote 49, *supra*.

[214] Donald J. Trump, March 27, 2020, Twitter,
https://twitter.com/realdonaldtrump/status/1243557418556162
050

[215] Orion Rummler, "Trump invokes DPA to target
"wartime profiteers" of medical equipment, AXIOS, April 4,
2020, https://www.axios.com/coronavirus-trump-dpa-medical-
masks-b756d07f-cb32-4f3c-815b-fcba8df77d27.html

216 Gavin Bade, "Trump expands DPA, amid mounting

pressure," Politico, April 2, 2020,
https://www.politico.com/news/2020/04/02/trump-expands-dpa-order-162128

[217] See endnote 1, supra, at time 39:00 onward

[218] Lisa Schnirring, "China Releases Genetic Data on New Coronavirus, Now Deadly," Center for Infectious Disease Research and Policy, University of Minnesota, January 11, 2020, https://www.cidrap.umn.edu/news-perspective/2020/01/china-releases-genetic-data-new-coronavirus-now-deadly

[219] "Transcript: Scott Gottlieb discusses coronavirus on "Face the Nation," Face The Nation, CBS NEWS, April 12, 2020, https://www.cbsnews.com/news/transcript-scott-gottlieb-discusses-coronavirus-on-face-the-nation-april-12-2020/

[220] Mairead McArdle, "China Supplied Faulty Coronavirus Test Kits to Spain, Czech Republic," National Review, March 26, 2020, https://news.yahoo.com/china-supplied-faulty-coronavirus-test-162306412.html

[221] Robert P. Baird, "What Went Wrong with Coronavirus Testing in the U.S.," The New Yorker, March 16, 2020, https://www.newyorker.com/news/news-desk/what-went-wrong-with-coronavirus-testing-in-the-us

[222] Roni Caryn Rabin, "C.D.C. Confirms First Possible Community Transmission of Coronavirus in U.S.," New York Times, February 26, 2020, https://www.nytimes.com/2020/02/26/health/coronavirus-cdc-usa.html

[223] Coronavirus Disease 2019 (COVID-19), Centers for Disease Prevention and Control, https://www.cdc.gov/coronavirus/2019-ncov/cases-updates/testing-in-us.html

[224] Nathaniel Weixel, "Alarm Bells Ring Over Controversial COVID Testing," The Hill, May 2, 2020,

https://thehill.com/policy/healthcare/495772-alarm-bells-ring-over-controversial-covid-testing

[225] Arman Azad, "WHO and CDC Never Discussed Providing International Test Kits to the US, Global Health Agency Says," CNN News Health, March 18, 2020, https://www.cnn.com/2020/03/18/health/who-coronavirus-tests-cdc/index.html

[226] "Biden falsely says Trump administration rejected WHO coronavirus test kits (that were never offered)," POLITIFACT, https://www.politifact.com/factchecks/2020/mar/16/joe-biden/biden-falsely-says-trump-administration-rejected-w/

[227] Nathaniel Weixel, "Trump health officials deny that US rejected WHO diagnostic test," The Hill, April 17, 2020, https://thehill.com/policy/healthcare/488076-trump-health-officials-deny-us-rejected-who-diagnostic-test

[228] Katy Reckdahl, Campbell Robertson and Richard Fausset, "New Orleans Faces a Virus Nightmare, and Mardi Gras May Be Why: Louisiana may be experiencing the world's fastest growth in new cases. Medical experts said Mardi Gras might have accelerated the crisis," New York Times, March 26, 2020, Updated April 13, 2020, https://www.nytimes.com/2020/03/26/us/coronavirus-louisiana-new-orleans.html

[229] "New Orleans Mardi Gras 2020," Louisiana Office of Tourism, https://www.louisianatravel.com/articles/new-orleans-mardi-gras-2020

[230] Death rates from coronavirus (COVID-19) in the United States as of August 18, 2020, by state, Statistia https://www.statista.com/statistics/1109011/coronavirus-covid19-death-rates-us-by-state/

[231] Lisette Voytko, "U.S. Coronavirus Outbreak Primarily Spread From New York City, Research Indicates," Forbes, May 7, 2020, https://www.forbes.com/sites/lisettevoytko/2020/05/07/us-

coronavirus-outbreak-likely-spread-from-new-york-city-research-indicates/#5e51b75d6152

232 Philip Sherwell (Bangkok), "Chinese Scientists Destroyed Proof of Virus in December," The Sunday Times, March 1, 2020, https://www.thetimes.co.uk/article/chinese-scientists-destroyed-proof-of-virus-in-december-rz055qjnj

233 Philip Sherwell (Bangkok), "Chinese scientists destroyed proof of virus in December," The Sunday Times, March 1, 2020, https://www.thetimes.co.uk/article/chinese-scientists-destroyed-proof-of-virus-in-december-rz055qjnj?ref=tokendaily

234 Shengjie Lai, Nick W Ruktanonchai, Liangcai Zhou, Olivia Prosper, Wei Luo, Jessica R Floyd, Amy Wesolowski, Mauricio Santillana, Chi Zhang, Xiangjun Du, Hongjie Yu, Andrew J Tatem, "Effect of non-pharmaceutical interventions for containing the COVID-19 outbreak in China," MedRxiv, March 13, 2020, https://www.medrxiv.org/content/10.1101/2020.03.03.20029843v2.

235 Peter Singer, "How China Is Working to Quarantine the Truth About the Coronavirus," Defense One, February 9, 2020. https://www.defenseone.com/ideas/2020/02/how-china-working-quarantine-truth-about-coronavirus/162985/

236 CNN Wire, "Beijing imposes restrictions on coronavirus research amid U.S.-China dispute on virus origin," KTLA TV News, April 13, 2020, https://ktla.com/news/nationworld/beijing-imposes-restrictions-on-coronavirus-research-amid-u-s-china-row-on-virus-origin/

237 Shengjie Lai, Nick W Ruktanonchai, Liangcai Zhou, Olivia Prosper, Wei Luo, Jessica R Floyd, Amy Wesolowski, Mauricio Santillana, Chi Zhang, Xiangjun Du, Hongjie Yu, Andrew J Tatem, "Effect of non-pharmaceutical interventions for containing the COVID-19 outbreak in China," March 13, 2020, doi: https://doi.org/10.1101/2020.03.03.20029843, https://www.medrxiv.org/content/10.1101/2020.03.03.200298

43v3, downloadable at
https://www.medrxiv.org/content/10.1101/2020.03.03.200298
43v3.full.pdf

[238] "Early and combined interventions crucial in tackling
Covid-19 spread in China," University of Southampton,
March 11, 2020,
https://www.southampton.ac.uk/news/2020/03/covid-19-
china.page. Published article accessible at
https://www.medrxiv.org/content/10.1101/2020.03.03.200298
43v2.

[239] Irwin Cotler [Chair of the Raoul Centre for Human
Rights, Emeritus Professor of Law at McGill University, and
former Minister of Justice and Attorney General of Canada]
and Judith Abitan [Executive Director of the Raoul
Wallenberg Centre for Human Rights, and a Human Rights
Advocate], "Xi Jinping's China did this," The Times of Israel,
April 12, 2020, https://www.timesofisrael.com/criminality-
and-corruption-reign-in-xi-pings-china/

[240] Rebeccah Heinrichs, "Five lies China is telling about
coronavirus," The Washington Examiner, April 15, 2020,
https://www.washingtonexaminer.com/opinion/five-lies-
china-is-telling-about-coronavirus

[241] CNN Wire, endnote 236, *supra.*

[242] Gerry Shih, Emily Rauhala and Lena H. Sun, "Early
Missteps and State Secrecy in China Probably Allowed the
Corona virus to Spread Farther and Faster," The Washington
Post, February 1, 2020,
https://www.washingtonpost.com/world/2020/02/01/early-
missteps-state-secrecy-china-likely-allowed-coronavirus-
spread-farther-faster/

[243] Leslie Eastman, "Report: China Destroyed Evidence of
Wuhan Coronavirus in December," Legal Insurrection, March
19, 2020, https://legalinsurrection.com/2020/03/report-china-
destroyed-evidence-of-wuhan-coronavirus-in-december/

[244] Bethany Allen-Ebrahimian, "Timeline: The early days

of China's coronavirus outbreak and cover-up," Axios, March 18, 2020, https://www.axios.com/timeline-the-early-days-of-chinas-coronavirus-outbreak-and-cover-up-ee65211a-afb6-4641-97b8-353718a5faab.html

[245] "Action by China would have curbed coronavirus cases by 95%, says study Communist officials destroyed evidence, suppressed news in early weeks," World Net Daily, March 19, 2020, https://www.wnd.com/2020/03/study-action-china-curbed-coronavirus-cases-95/

[246] "Wuhan's so-called wet markets are back in business, ABC News, April 15, 2020, https://abcnews.go.com/International/wuhans-called-wet-markets-back-business/story?id=70119116

[247] Gerry Shih, Emily Rauhala and Lena H. Sun, "Early missteps and state secrecy in China probably allowed the coronavirus to spread farther and faster, *The Washington Post*, February 1, 2020, https://www.washingtonpost.com/world/2020/02/01/early-missteps-state-secrecy-china-likely-allowed-coronavirus-spread-farther-faster/

[248] Beth Baumann, "WHO's Senior Advisor Had an Astonishing Response When Asked About Taiwan," Townhall, March 28, 2020, https://townhall.com/tipsheet/bethbaumann/2020/03/28/watch-whos-senior-advisor-hangs-up-on-a-reporter-for-asking-about-taiwan-n2565899

[249] Helen Raleigh, "Coronavirus and China's Missing Journalists," *National Review*, March 19, 2020, https://www.nationalreview.com/magazine/2020/04/06/coronavirus-and-chinas-missingcitizen-journalists/

[250] Joshua Phillips, "Coronavirus – The Lies and the Truth," video documentary, *The Epoch Times*, https://www.youtube.com/watch?v=hSIt496d82s

[251] See also, "Programming Alert: Exclusive Documentary on Origin of the CCP Virus Premieres," Epoch Times, April 7,

2020, updated on April 12, 2020,
https://www.theepochtimes.com/programming-alert-
exclusive-documentary-on-origin-of-the-ccp-virus-
premieres_3302336.html

Made in the USA
Middletown, DE
04 January 2021

30846604R00144